Shakira

Woman Full Of Grace

Ximena Diego

Translation by
Francheska Farinacci

WITHDRAWN

A FIRESIDE BOOK

PUBLISHED BY SIMON & SCHUSTER

NEW YORK • LONDON • TORONTO • SYDNEY • SINGAPORE

FIRESIDE
Rockefeller Center
1230 Avenue of the Americas
New York, NY 10020

FIRESIDE and colophon are registered trademarks of
Simon & Schuster, Inc.

Designed by BTDnyc
PRODUCED BY K&N BOOKWORKS INC.

Manufactured in the United States of America
10 9 8 7 6 5 4 3 2 1

Library of Congress Cataloging-in-Publication Data is available.

ISBN 0-7432-1623-7

ACKNOWLEDGMENTS

For this book I collected newspaper articles, interviews, anecdotes, and the stories of the people who have accompanied Shakira throughout her career. Along the way I met people who were very generous with their time and their memories. To all of them, my sincere thanks. Among those who made this book possible are Alexi Castillo, director of *TV y Novelas* in Colombia; María del Rosario Sánchez, Shakira's first manager; Michelle Hustik, the president of her fan club in Bogotá; Brendan Buckley, a drummer who accompanies Shakira; Luis Fernando Ochoa, composer and producer; César Navarro, one of her dancers during the *Magia* period; Carlos Venegas, a promoter who watched her grow; Jairo Martínez, of Estefan Enterprises; and Carlos Muñoz, of Sony Colombia. Thanks to Estela Bolaños for being an ideal daughter of Barranquilla and to Noelia, in Buenos Aires, for keeping updated one of the best Web sites on Shakira (www.shakiramebarak.com). After I talked to all of these people and others who were part of her life, after I read and watched interviews, listened to her music, visited Internet sites, and talked to her fans, this book was born. It aims to be more than just a summary, which would always be incomplete, of the events that formed Shakira. I hope to have shed some light on the history of this singer-songwriter who, beyond fashion and awards, is transforming the music scene with the force of an earthquake and promises to become the most successful crossover act in history.

My thanks to the executives at Simon & Schuster, especially my editor, Marcela Landres, who shepherded and supported this project so well, and to my literary agent Laura Dail, who recommended me for the task and who was always close by during the research and writing. I would also like to thank Dolores Prida for her valuable help and wise advice, and Francheska Farinacci for her fine translation. Finally, I would like to thank my adoring family for their constant love.

TO MARK,

for making sense of what surrounds me.

Contents

SHAKIRA

INTRODUCTION

When Shakira arrived at the first annual Latin Grammy Awards in Los Angeles, with her blonde hair and a green dress, some of the people attending had barely heard of her. But by the end of the night those same people would remember her forever. All she had to do was step on stage and give that defiant look with her gypsy eyes while moving her hips sensually to the rhythm of the dumbek, the drum of her ancestors, to take over the audience. Nobody could take their eyes off this woman who seemed possessed by ancient spirits and sang in Arabic with the voice of a veteran rocker. That night, Shakira made it clear why *Time* magazine had put her on the cover above the headline "Era of the Rockera," why Gabriel García Márquez had interviewed her for his publication *Cambio*, and why she has sold millions of records worldwide.

But who is this young Colombian with the Arabic name ? Who is this performer who belly dances and composes, who can sell out stadiums and launch fashion trends? Before 2001, few of us in the United States knew who she was, but throughout Latin America, Europe, the Middle East, and even Japan, her songs have repeatedly reached number one and her videos have occupied the top spots on MTV for months. To many, she is the undisputed queen of pop and rock *en español*.

When this blazing hurricane began to sell millions of records, the critics were stunned and spat out comparisons to Alanis Morissette and Janis Joplin. And while the three have comparable hairstyles, passion, and vocal styles, Shakira's spirit is far removed from politics, depression, and the psychedelic. Her personality, it must be said, is not simple. She is extremely spiritual, a dreamer and happy, almost childlike. And yet her wisdom and intuition make her seem more of an old soul, a woman who has lived other lives and knows where to go and how to get there —as if her destiny were already set.

She is extremely charismatic, and it's clear that her parents were not mistaken when they baptized her Shakira, which in Arabic means "woman full of grace" and in Hindi, "goddess of light." Through her Lebanese blood came artistic karma, and at four years old she surprised everyone when she began to belly dance without ever having been taught. At the age of eight she composed her first song, and five years later she signed her first record contract, with Sony Colombia no less, to record an album of her own songs.

Success with a capital *S* came to her at nineteen, when in December of 1995 her third album, *Pies descalzos (Bare Feet)*, put her voice on the radio all over the planet, literally: the song "Estoy aquí" ("I Am Here") played from Buenos Aires to Tokyo, and Brazil and Turkey in between. The next record, *Dónde están los ladrones? (Where Are the Thieves?)*, which came with the patronage of Emilio Estefan Jr., confirmed her status as an artist and proved that she was no one-hit wonder. On the contrary, a month after its launch, the record had already sold over a million copies. A few months later, MTV opened the doors of its studios and asked her to do an acoustic concert, the famous *Unplugged* series, while she made plans for her next album in English. Impressive.

Success did not come overnight for Shakira. The road was cluttered with barriers, bumps, and steep hills, but she also found many allies, and she served as her own very first one. Ironically, Shakira never joined her school choir: the music teacher said her voice sounded like the bleating of a goat. In perhaps, the first blow to her artistic pride, she said nothing in class; she waited until she got home to cry, so no one could see her. A couple of weeks later, she returned to class with her first trophies won at a talent competition. The awards began to accumulate, and the day after each victory, without fail, Shakira would take her trophy to school and show it off in front of that teacher.

Shakira's first break came when she impressed a Sony Colombia executive, singing and belly dancing, in the hallway of a hotel. As a result, she got her first record contract. And a few years later, when her label was considering terminating her contract, Shakira shut everyone up with *Pies descalzos*. With the same faith and perseverance that years before she had used to dominate talent competitions, she now amassed gold and platinum records, to brandish before those executives who in the past had made her life impossible.

Her talent is undeniable and innate, but on the way to fame she also always found the allies her career needed. With uncommonly keen instinct for a teenager, she was able to contact the right people. She got the support of an entertainment magazine, *TV y Novelas*, and a manager Patricia Téllez who gave her the support of Caracol Televisión, the most prestigious TV producer in Colombia at that time. She knew how to make the most of her budding popularity in Latin America and enter the American market holding the hand of Emilio Estefan Jr. first, and Freddie DeMann later. The latter, who once handled Madonna's and Michael Jackson's careers, currently manages Shakira. Without a doubt, this artist knows which coattails to grab on to, and from the beginning she has known exactly where she wanted to go.

These days, for example, searching for information about her past can be very difficult, since, for some reason, neither her Fan Club in Colombia, nor her ex-manager Patricia Téllez, nor her old friends in

Barranquilla want to talk about her to the press—according to some, it is the artist's explicit wish. But one story a *TV y Novelas* reporter tells is now ancient history: When Shakira first came to Bogotá from Barranquilla, she spent hours in the editorial room with nothing to do, just waiting for someone to interview her.

All in all, to most of the hundreds of reporters who have interviewed her in the course of her career, Shakira seems more like the girl next door than an international rock star. As she was before finding fame, Shakira remains a devout Catholic who goes to church and takes confession. However, she also continues to read atheistic writers (and never ceases to wonder why they don't attribute their inspiration to God) and thus keeps her intellect sharp and her imagination fertile. She is eclectic and loves it. "I'm a cocktail of elements," she has said proudly more than once.

She is physically small, no taller than 5'2". But once she takes the stage, her presence is monumental. She knows how to move on stage, how to speak to her audience, how to tease them. Her concerts are cathartic, the audience singing along from beginning to end; there is dancing, pushing, screaming, hysteria…. "Idol…" they scream to her.

The majority of her admirers, however, have never gone to any of her concerts. Her millions of fans worldwide meet on the Internet, where they converse in Turkish, Portuguese, English, Spanish, and French. The week that rumors first appeared about her romance with Antonio de la Rúa, the son of Argentina's president, Shakira's name was the sixth most popular word searched worldwide on the AltaVista portal.

Unlike the typical pop singers of her generation, Shakira writes and composes her own songs, she contributes to the arrangements, plays the guitar and harmonica, belly dances, and sings in Portuguese and now in English, as well as her native Spanish. Experienced, sensual, and wise, this artist is making her mark in the homogenous pop world. Perhaps the following pages will help us understand who this woman full of grace is, how she does it, and where she comes from.

1

BEGINNINGS

"Barranquilla is my land, my people, my family, my friends...."

"I am a walking contradiction. A mix of elements that come from far and different worlds." That was how our artist described herself a couple of years ago, and she went on to explain: "But these elements are not in conflict, they coexist peacefully. I accept all of the contradictions within me and they accept one another." And no city could better represent Shakira's soul than the city where she was born. Just like her persona, in Barranquilla disparate and distant elements coexist in harmony and mutual respect.

Bathed by the Caribbean waters and visited by almost countless merchants since the colonial era, Shakira's home is one of the most joyful and vibrant cities in Colombia. Barranquilla is the most important port in the country, through which tons of coffee and petroleum are imported and exported, and through which almost every race in the world has passed. Since its founding in the seventeenth century, the city has grown with a mixture of three races: the Indigenous, the Spaniard, and the African. But during the last one hundred years this area was the final destination of immigrants from various countries and cultures, among them German, Jewish, Italian, Irish, Chinese, Lebanese, and Palestinian. They settled peacefully, having nothing to lose just dreams to fulfill, in search of a better life. With time, these cultures began to settle in, leaving their marks in the architecture, the music, and the food, whether in the construction of a new synagogue, the proliferation of Chinese laundromats, or the aroma of fried arepas and barbecued sausages.

These communities began to expand and integrate, making this beautiful coastal region a privileged center that earned the nickname "the golden door" or "carrumba the beautiful," an imaginative city, economically active and tolerant of differences. "The Barranquillero is a simple, open, and hard-working person. He knows how to live life but isn't a fanatic. He won't kill himself over politics or religion....When it comes to soccer, however, they will kill anyone," joked one Caribbean Colombian in describing her people. "Barranquilla is a melting pot of many nationalities, which is why the people assimilate foreign cultures rather than fight them," she said.

No other event exhibits this cultural mix with as much splendor as Carnival: the ultimate party. Once a year, men, women, and children take to the streets dressed in colorful costumes and makeup for the parade of floats and to dance, to play the drums, and to celebrate rambunctiously in the purest Caribbean spirit. During Carnival, anything goes and the sky's the limit when it comes to the imagination: there are parodies and political satires, there are carnival queens and traditional songs....The days of Carnival are wild, the streets are packed, and no one is left out. During these four days, rich and poor are equals, and the only law is fun.

Religious festivals are celebrated with the same passion. Even though each religion celebrates in its own way, the majority of the population in Barranquilla is Catholic, and thousands of families get together to celebrate Christmas Eve, Christmas, and New Year's Day. Perhaps as another example of integration, the faith brought by the Spaniards is practiced today by members of other communities that were not Catholic originally, like much of the Arab community. This includes Shakira's family, who are Lebanese but practice the Catholic faith while retaining many of their Arabic customs, such as music and food.

Unlike Bogotá and Medellín, Barranquilla is a peaceful city that remains far removed from political intrigue and drug trafficking. Barranquilleros didn't experience the constant terrorist attacks and the political kidnapping that gave Colombia such a bad reputation, especially during the nineties. As if the closeness to the sea tamed the beast, Barranquilla did not have to endure the fear of the almost daily exploding car bombs or the horrendous assassinations of powerful officials. As many residents proudly point out about this city, Barranquilla is tolerant and "Caribbean."

Perhaps because of the latter, when this city is not working, it's partying or socializing till all hours of the night. Its residents live according to the city's own schedule, very calmly, as though savoring the day. After all, a large part of the year they live in a humid heat, more suitable for chatting while drinking a cool soda than working up a sweat while running for the bus.

In this privileged urban center, within the harsh reality of Colombia, Shakira Isabel Mebarak Ripoll was born on Wednesday, February 2, 1977, in the Clínica Asunción de Barranquilla. Daughter of a respected jeweler of Lebanese descent, Don William Mebarak Chadid, and his Colombian wife, Nidia Ripoll Torrado, the child was the couple's blessing and their only daughter. In naming the newborn, Nidia had shuffled through several names containing the letter "k" to go well with the sound of the "k" in Mebarak. She had considered Karime and Katiuska but finally chose Shakira, an Arabic name derived from the word *shukram*, which means "grace." The most literal translation is "woman full of grace," even though Shakira has said she identifies more with its second meaning, "grateful."

Colombians said that the newborn was chubby and had curly hair, thick eyebrows, and a healthy set of lungs. What nobody knew was that those lungs would inscribe her name in music history.

HER PEOPLE AND HER FAMILY

"I come from a traditional society, not only because I went to a Catholic school, but because I was raised in a house that is half Arabic and half Barranquillera, in a small coastal city."

According to Colombian reporters, Don William Esteban Mebarak Chadid was born in New York City, but shortly after he was born his family moved to Barranquilla. Nidia Ripoll Torrado, on the other hand, was born in Barranquilla and has Catalan blood. When they married Don William was divorced and already had seven children from his previous marriage. So Shakira came into this world as the youngest child with quite a few siblings willing to spoil her.

Don William has been a key figure in Shakira's formation and sensibility. Proud of his Lebanese roots, he was a professional jeweler and a vocational writer. According to the magazine *TV y Novelas* Colombia, during his days as a jeweler he built his clientele and was able to maintain a jewelry store in Barranquilla for almost two decades. But shortly after Shakira was born he had already liquidated that business and was just selling watches close to where he lived. Nidia was the homemaker and by closely minding her daughter, she was the one who first suspected the little one's artistic tendencies.

Don William's passion for literature and all things intellectual and artistic made Shakira grow up surrounded by all kinds of books and Arabic music, but it may have been because of Nidia's religious fervor that the child came to know the Bible. In Shakira's own words, her parents are very different but complement each other: "My father is idealistic, my mother realistic, and because of that, in my home I find both earth and air. My father is the insanity and my mother the sanity."

For many years the couple belonged to a social club where the families of the Lebanese community would get together and enjoy their traditions through food, dance, and music. This was one of the places where the Mebarak family socialized and it is where Shakira began to taste Arabic dishes and observe from a young age how the hips of the dancers moved.

The Mebaraks made a good living. They were a middle-class family able to send their only daughter to a good Catholic school and to pay for private lessons in singing, modern dancing, and modeling. They kept a nice house in the northern part of Barranquilla and had the luxuries of a family that knew how to make the best of simple things. But beyond material abundance, William and Nidia raised their daughter with Christian values and were attentive to her every need: they knew how to listen to the desires of the restless and curious child and quickly realized that she would not have an ordinary life.

When Shakira was a child, Nidia discovered that she had a gift for writing. According to Colombian columnists, the child knew the alphabet by the age of eighteen months, at three she knew how to read, and by the time she was four she was ready for school. It seemed as though she might have been a child prodigy. At least that's what Nidia believed, so she had her academically tested to determine if the little girl was a genius.

Shakira lived alone with her parents, though it was quite frequent for her half siblings to come over, be it to baby-sit or to play with her, since they lived only a few blocks away. That may be why when Shakira talks about her family she includes her brothers and sisters (omitting the "half") as well as her parents. Of all her father's children, Shakira never met her oldest half brother, because he died before she was born. Her oldest sister, Lucy, is a surgeon living in Colombia, like most of her siblings. Next is Alberto, a lawyer who lives in Barranquilla and got married in January 2001. Moisés, also married, is the third child. Tonino is the fourth child and the closest to Shakira, having worked for many years as her road manager. Tonino was going to follow in his father's footsteps but found that Shakira's success promised him a more entertaining career. He is married and has a little girl who is Shakira's goddaughter. "As the youngest, she is the pampered one in the family. She's not spoiled but knows exactly what she is doing and has a great disposition," he told a Colombian magazine a few years ago.

Following Tonino is Patricia, who lives in Spain and is a special education teacher. And finally, there is Antonio and Edward, the youngest, who lives in Miami.

Probably because of her Catholic upbringing or having grown up among so much affection, *family* has a sacred meaning to Shakira. She is extremely proud of her family nucleus, an entity that gives her strength and joy, the circle that nourishes her during her moments of searching. Asked about their family dynamics, Don William seized the opportunity to speak of Shakira's generosity with her brothers and sister: "She paid for Lucy's medical school, she pays Edward's schooling in the United States, she bought Alberto a car, and she employed Tonino as her representative."

But before she came into the active and complex existence she has today, Shakira's childhood was tranquil, filled with the adventures and discoveries of just another Barranquillera.

A Childhood between the Neighborhood and the Beach

"I remember having very loving parents, with whom I always had great communication. I remember that I would pray to God singing."

The Mebaraks lived in a neighborhood called El Limoncito, a safe family suburb where people knew one another by name. In the afternoons the boys would play soccer in the streets and the girls would get together on the sidewalks, or mixed groups would play cops and robbers. Sometimes they would simply be in one another's houses doing one of the numerous activities that children do when they have their whole lives in front of them.

Shakira's childhood was full of strong relationships with neighbors and friends, some of which have lasted. In fact today when she is asked if she has many friends she always and frankly answers no, that she could count all of her friends on just one hand and they are the same ones she had when she was growing up in Barranquilla. In her neighborhood she built relationships that have lasted years, and she is still friends with some of her neighbors to this day.

One of her best friends while growing up was Vanesa Vengoechea, who was interviewed years ago by *TV y Novelas*. When they were children they used to play in the street, get ready for parties together, and watch movies at each other's houses. She remembers it was rare to see Shakira sad. She was very good at listening to problems and giving advice, Vanesa told a Colombian magazine, but even though they both would talk a lot about their issues, what they loved most was going out. "Our favorite plans were going to the beach or playing volleyball," she said. On the weekends they would meet at Vanesa's house to watch movies until late into the night. Among Shakira's favorite movies were horror flicks: she loved to be scared half to death. The problem, said Vanesa, was that Shakira would always talk during the movie, making some sort of observation. "And when it was over she would want to talk about the plot, but rarely found anyone up for it." Restless and articulate, Shakira always had something to say.

The little Mebarak loved carnivals, dances, french fries, Coca-Cola, and the patacones (fried plantains) that "El Viejo Paco" fired up at the Vengoecheas' house. According to Paola, Vanesa's sister, Shakira loved parties, but other than Óscar, her first boyfriend, no one liked to go with her, because "Doña Nidia made her come home early, before midnight." According to this family, our artist remains unchanged, just as simple and happy as before. However, now when she stops by for a visit, she wears a wig and dark glasses to prevent her fans from recognizing her.

The rest of her neighbors who still live in El Limoncito also remember her as happy and lively, regularly sitting on her doorstep with her guitar. "She never took off her uniform when she got home from school, but she did take off her socks and shoes. Sometimes you would see her walking barefoot alone around the block and other times with her group of friends."

Like every good coastal girl, Shakira spent much of her time outside. "I would play with boys and that helped me in the long run, because in this career one has to deal with a lot of men," she acknowledged years later.

To find the more feminine side of Shakira, one would have to go inside her house. In her room she played with dolls like any girl her age. While she made up stories about her dolls, her father would recreate other ones. As an avid lover of music and of words, Don William spent a great part of his day in front of his typewriter creating stories and poems. And even though he was in his own world, Shakira would observe him without missing a detail. "The image of him writing was so strong," said Shakira as an adult, "that I wanted to be like him." And that was how she started to imitate him, first in her gestures, and later mentally: starting a short time after learning how to write, she would lock herself in her room, surrounded by teddy bears and dolls, and write poetic passages that she would later recite to her parents.

In addition to her father's example, Shakira's mind was nourished by the stories her mother read to her as a child and the books she started reading as soon as she was able. Her first book was *Treasure Island* by Robert Louis Stevenson, a gift from her father. One can only imagine the fantasies that this story might have awakened in the adventurous mind of this child from the Caribbean Sea. But the book she talks about most is *The Prophet* by the Lebanese Kahlil Gibran, which she says has influenced her profoundly. The third book that Shakira remembers from her childhood is the Bible. And not just from parochial school; Nidia read the Bible every single day, and this had a lasting influence on Shakira.

Accompanying these books were the sounds of records playing in her home. In addition to the Arabic music that her father played, she listened to Donna Summer and Miguel Bosé. Not only did she admire Miguel Bosé's voice, he "was like my platonic love," she said later. She adored the lyrics of his songs and felt that love that is inspired by singers when their music reaches the heart of listeners.

So this is how Shakira grew up: in a room filled with Barbie dolls and teddy bears, as well as a guitar and a volleyball. In a corner of that same room she prepared a workstation, with a little chair and a table, so she could sit comfortably as she composed her poems. From the time she was four years old, her hours were spent at school, the beach, and parties, between the street and her house or her friends' houses, surrounded by coastal scents, a mixture of salty air and ripe pineapples. Between the sand and the sea, facing a distant horizon that one day she would go out and conquer.

DISCOVERING HER CALLING

"The nuns were very open-minded, at least to the extent that their environment allowed it...."

By the time she was two years old, Shakira already knew the alphabet, and by three, she already knew how to write more that her name, but the law did not permit her to begin school at such a young age. However, as soon as she turned four, this mischievous and restless little person began preschool in one of the most prestigious institutions in the city.

La Enseñanza de Barranquilla, a traditional school in the city founded and administered by missionary nuns from the Order of Mary, was not just where Shakira learned her arithmetic and her geography, but also where she began to learn the Catholic faith, a cornerstone of her formation. In these cloisters, between religion classes and drawing assignments, between numbers and vowels, the tiny hurricane began to discover aspects of her personality that she did not know existed—or rather, that nobody knew existed.

Because she was short, Shakira was always the first in any line. She loved that because she loved attention, and that was the easiest way to get it. But shortly after starting school, she found a more original and legitimate way to become the center of attention. As she often says, dancing was her first way of expressing herself. "My first encounter with dance was when I was four years old and I began to belly dance." What is curious is that no one had taught her. "It's proof that a collective, genetic memory really does exist, because as long as I've been aware, as soon as I hear the beat of a derbeque my hips begin to move instantly, without any effort at all."

This episode, which Shakira now describes calmly, astonished her parents and her teachers. No one had ever taught her how to do the

Arab dance, but her sixth sense incorporated what she had seen in the Arabic social club where she used to go with her family. That Friday, when she danced in front of her schoolmates, her teachers, and her mother, she discovered her inner diva and saw that she had a captive audience. She enjoyed moving her diminutive hips to the Eastern rhythms so much that every Friday she would do the same number religiously in a civic show held by the school. The draw that the stage had for the little dancer was uncontrollable, and fortunately no one tried to stop her—though she now recalls, between laughs, that she bored her schoolmates practically to tears.

The truth was that beyond the dance, what Shakira was looking for was attention. And however she got it was fine. "I had the profound need to be noticed," she concluded later.

Even though Shakira got good grades in school, she was not a star student. "In school Shakira was sensible and disciplined, but also absentminded," recalled María Claudia Manotas, another old friend, who is now an audiologist. "Sometimes in class she just didn't pay attention. She immersed herself in writing lyrics on the back of her notebook. But even so, she had the capacity to catch on to everything very quickly, because whenever the teacher would catch her, she would look up at the board and almost immediately figure out where we were." She goes on to say, "Recess was sacred to Shakira: as soon as the bell rang she was the first one to run and get in line for the cafeteria. I remember her drinking Pepsi with a pastry with dulce de leche….But she got annoyed if you asked her for some."

Back then, the little girl dreamed of becoming an astronaut and working for NASA. Though she had a reputation for daydreaming, Shakira was very aware of what was happening around her. She was intuitive and even had a head for business. She would never go hungry, as they say. Don William, who attributes that talent to her Lebanese blood, said one day, "When she was a child she made a handwritten newspaper, which she designed on her own with gossip from school. She sold it to her classmates until one day one of the nuns discovered it and confiscated the copies!"

While this anecdote describes the sixth sense that she was already developing for business, Shakira was not destined to become a newspaper reporter or a businesswoman. Back then no one knew what she would become, not even her mother, who watched her development more closely than anyone. Ever since her daughter started to belly dance Nidia knew that she was raising someone out of the ordinary. "She started to become obsessed with science, she ended up convincing us that she might become a researcher," says Nidia. "But then she would lock herself in the room day and night, writing stories and poems. She tricked us again when we thought we might have a writer for a daughter. But then I discovered that the writer part was just the first step, and what she was writing was the lyrics to her songs."

The fact that the child had an artistic vocation was very clear. The same artistic blood that expressed itself for the first time in belly dance returned to knock on the doors of her imagination when she learned to write. Wanting to imitate her father, she would lock herself in her room with pen and paper and write. She wrote stories and poems, always in the same corner of her room, in that workstation she had prepared, and always with the same concentration. No one really knew what Shakira was writing about, but a few times, after being locked up for hours, the budding author would go to her parents and read them her work. And they always listened.

Shakira admired her father and imitated him. But there was something else in the figure of her father that she could not understand. And this had to do not with his vocation as a writer but with something much more physical.

Don William wore sunglasses that were not only dark but also particularly big, and to a little girl, huge. Seeing her father hide behind those big glasses so impressed Shakira that she decided to exorcise her fear in a song. And thus, "Tus gafas oscuras" ("Your Dark Glasses") was born, her first poem set to music. With the ingenuity of someone trying to solve a mystery and find hidden treasure, Shakira discovered that she could write songs. "At the age of eight I discovered that poetry and music make the perfect marriage," she now recalls. That day when she wrote her first song, the muse had been her father. But after this first step, her muses were now in the street, in life, and in her reflections. After that first encounter, Shakira found inspiration in many people and events, in falling in love and, above all, in falling out of love.

After "Tus gafas oscuras" another song came, and a few months later another one, and then another. In school, at the beach, or walking by herself through the neighborhood, barefoot and still in her uniform, words, phrases and ideas came to her. Later on she would lock herself in her room and put them to music with her guitar.

Around then, it began to dawn on Nidia that the child had talent and had to channel it in some form. Nidia's intuition was on target: this little girl was an artist. And her talents were not limited to the belly dancing she'd been doing since age four. Here is where Nidia's role becomes crucial in Shakira's future: without letting much time go by, she took her daughter to her first singing lessons and became the person who most encouraged her.

In addition to her education and voice training, Shakira began to fashion her body for the stage. When she was ten Nidia enrolled her in an academy in Barranquilla called Passarela for her first modeling course. She learned how to apply her own makeup, fix her hair, and walk gracefully. She also took classes in modern dance and movement. As she made new friends she got a taste of what life was like for children who train from a young age to be famous. That was also where Shakira learned the importance of aesthetics. There she learned how to smile for the camera and maintain her posture, to pay attention to her clothes, and to take care of her body. And perhaps it was during her days at Passarela that she acquired the habit of being extremely careful about her image when photographed.

But not everything was a lesson for the young artist. By the end of her first decade, the little girl began to put into practice everything she had learned inside the four walls of her classrooms. Around the time she was attending classes at Passarela, she was already dancing in various places, and her parents were acting as her managers. They both, but especially Nidia, encouraged her to participate in her first singing competition. When she turned ten she won her first trophy, and from then on there wasn't a competition that Shakira would miss, whether in school or on stage, before television cameras or away from them. If Nidia or William could take her, the little girl was there. And frequently, Shakira came home with a trophy.

This small competitive circuit that Nidia and Shakira entered when the little girl was just ten years old formed the foundation of her career. This was not only because Shakira was infatuated with the stage and was discovering herself as an artist, but also because she was making her first contacts inside the industry.

Mother and daughter would roam the hallways of television studios, knocking on doors and getting in line for auditions. According to people who knew Shakira in the beginning, no one had as much faith in her as her parents. If Don William was her intellectual guide in songwriting, Doña Nidia was her spiritual mentor. It was her perseverance that opened doors for Shakira. As the artist said, "My mother was a driving force. She detected my restlessness and stimulated it." Her mother was attentive to the artistic talent that her daughter was demonstrating, first in dance, then in writing, and later on in music. As soon as she realized that she had an extraordinary child, Nidia encouraged her to develop her talents. As in the Bible's parable of talents, Nidia was stimulating her into multiplying and sharing them. And that is precisely what Shakira is doing today.

THE FIRST FRUSTRATION

Though Shakira's talent was undeniable to the Mebaraks, there was one person who did not agree. It was none other than Shakira's music teacher, a man that Shakira would remember her whole life. When Shakira attended elementary school she tried to join the school choir. However, when the choir members were chosen, Shakira was left out. The reason? According to the teacher, her voice was like the "bleating of a goat" and threw the group off key.

This incident affected Shakira greatly. That day in school she didn't say a word, as if she didn't care. But when she got home she cried, angry and hurt. Her artistic pride had taken a blow just when she was getting started. Luckily, she could turn to her parents, who believed in her talent. They consoled her and cheered her up that night. But even back then, Shakira could count on a virtue that she still possesses: determination. She wanted to sing, and no one was going to stop her. She was going to show that teacher who Shakira was.

The singing and modeling classes were helpful when it came to facing new audiences, especially outside of school. When Shakira performed in youth competitions, her vibrato voice, which had annoyed the music teacher so greatly, was a revelation to the judges. It was an original compared to the soft voices of the other elementary-school girls and boys. With her raw talent on the stage, Shakira won her first trophy at the age of ten and her first major local trophy a year later.

This last one was an award from the television show "Vivan los niños," where Shakira competed against other young talents from around the country. Far from being a frivolous, local competition, this competition was broadcast in various cities on the station Telecaribe of Colombia. And when Shakira returned to compete the following two years, she won first prize two more times. In between, the Barranquillera also competed in the Niña Atlántico beauty contest, where her little face and style earned her the place of first runner-up.

During those years of early success and local recognition, Shakira never forgot the music teacher. After each triumph, she would take her trophy to school and invariably parade it in front of him.

When she started being famous outside of school, the music teacher asked her to join the school choir. She said no. She never did join the choir.

2

IN SEARCH OF
A DREAM

"I always dreamed of the stars...."

THE FIRST RECORD CONTRACT

After she had won several competitions and performed at local universities, Shakira's fame began to spread. Her name had been printed in the newspapers, her smiling face was featured in several magazines, and she had even appeared on television more than once. Not bad for a twelve-year-old.

The young girl was beginning to make a name for herself thanks to her undeniable talent and, more than anything, her dedication. On the child actor's circuit, Shakira met Mónica Ariza, the producer of a theater group called "Los Monachos." Being in the business, Ariza was used to seeing gifted kids, but she couldn't help but be impressed by Shakira's talent and tenacity. In the few times she'd seen her, the producer realized that the young girl had the talent and the charisma necessary to make it far. So when she found out that a promoter for the record company Sony Colombia, an acquaintance of hers, was coming to town to promote a couple of vallenato groups, she didn't hesitate for a second. She called him and insisted that he see Shakira. She spoke so highly about this "child genius," who composed, sang, and also danced, that the executive gave in, granting her an audition in the hotel where he was staying.

As soon as she got the okay for this less than conventional audition, Mónica Ariza contacted Nidia Mebarak and suggested she take her daughter by the hotel before the promoter returned to Bogotá. That very day Shakira went out in search of her destiny accompanied by her mother, with a homemade demo tape in hand. She introduced herself to the Sony Music promoter, Mr. Ciro Vargas, who had heard so much about the talents of this young girl that he was curious to see what all the fuss was about. And when he finally saw her, he got it. That afternoon in the hallway of the El Prado Hotel, Shakira sang a capella and danced to one of the songs in her repertoire. And what had drawn applause from previous audiences ended up working on this man, too.

Ciro Vargas was impressed. He was so surprised by what he had heard that he kept the homemade recording and set up a live second audition, but this time in front of other company executives, in the central offices in Bogotá. A couple of days later Shakira, Nidia, and William Mebarak arrived in the capital of Colombia, where Shakira performed a song and dance routine behind the closed doors of a dance club for the top Sony executives. As always her belly dance was incorporated into her routine along with a song of her own making. The little girl sang on the dance floor and danced the only way she knew how.

Even though the executives were not overly impressed with her voice, which at the time was underdeveloped, there was something in the way she presented herself, her outgoing attitude and her self-confidence, that compelled the executives to make her an offer. She had all the qualities of an up-and-coming star. A couple of weeks later a lucky thirteen-year-old Barranquillera with an Arabic name was signing, with her parents as managers, her first record contract. And she was doing it with Sony Records, the most internationally renowned label.

The contract between Shakira and Sony was for three records. To Sony this was a relatively low-budget project that didn't require much production, but they knew they were dealing with a diamond in the rough. At that time, though, no one knew if this precious stone would ever be polished.

Magia and Her First Kiss

By the end of her childhood with adolescence knocking on her door, Shakira was becoming a professional musician. Her teen years were still to come, yet she could already boast a record contract. Schoolwork started to alternate with rehearsals and meetings with the Sony producers. Her love for music had finally morphed into something tangible: her first record.

Sony had offered Shakira a contract for three albums, but the record company would have full control. Shakira did not determine the concept of the first album, but it had a style that molded itself around her personality: it had a lot of love ballads and a little dance music. Accompanying the diminutive diva would be four backup dancers at every performance. That was a suggestion from Shakira that the record company agreed to incorporate for the launch of the album in various cities.

The dancers, who were chosen by audition, also had to know how to sing, since they would perform the chorus and any masculine voices. César Navarro, Guillermo Gómez, Mauricio Pinilla, and Richard Ricardo were chosen. Like Shakira, they were all from Barranquilla and two of them had attended the Academia de Modelaje Passarela. As such, there was a good working environment and good communication among the five of them.

As soon as her team was chosen, they all began to take dance classes with two well-known choreographers, Gary Julio and Ray Silva, and a couple of months before the record was launched they started rehearsing. According to one of them, César Navarro, who was also her leading man in the video for"Magia," Shakira was unstoppable. When everyone was finished rehearsing, Shakira would stay behind to practice the movements over and over or to do some sort of exercise routine. "Those of us who knew her at that time," says César, "we'd say, 'huh, this girl is going to make it far.' She had an incredible talent, she composed easily, she was extremely sensitive, affectionate, and tender."

Shakira would go to the rehearsals dressed comfortably, in shorts and a T-shirt or, if there was no time to change, in her school uniform. Often she had to finish her homework after rehearsals. But she had enough energy for everything: school, rehearsals, homework, and singing lessons. The little girl was living her dream, and no one was going to wake her up. She was happy. After almost three months of preproduction, working with the songs and rehearsing the choreography, she recorded *Magia*, an album comprised of eight songs she had written between the ages of eight and twelve.

According to one Sony Colombia executive, the recording process was simple and problem free, though he adds that Shakira was quite hardheaded and fairly capricious. For the young artist, the process was problematic, because she was not included in choosing the rhythms or the songs. Everything about the overall artistic production of the material was decided without her input—something she did not like at all. Shakira had written the songs, or at least the first drafts. How much the material was altered, only she knows. The artistic production of the album was completely in the hands of the producers, Miguel E. Cubillo and Pablo Tedeschi. According to statements the latter made to the Colombian magazine *Semana*, Shakira was like an adult in a child's body. "Even though she was under the recording company's control, she knew what she wanted," he said.

With *Magia*, which from the start was allotted a low budget, Shakira had a good first record that demonstrated her indisputable potential. As if reflecting her preadolescence, the themes of her songs ranged from a poem to her prince charming in "Sueños," to a celebration of dance in "Esta noche voy contigo." In this lineup Shakira covered the entire catalog of emotions that spring from being in love for the first time. Except for "Tus gafas oscuras," all the songs speak to the man–prince charming with whom she was in love.

These themes contained the freshness of her first experiences with the opposite sex, the influences of the adventure stories that her father used to give her, and the dreams of a young coastal girl.

Not coincidentally, during the preproduction of the first album, Shakira was discovering love. It was no longer the platonic love she'd had for Miguel Bosé. Now she had a real boyfriend from her neighborhood, and she was feeling firsthand the emotions she was singing about in her love songs. Óscar Pardo, who lived across the street from her, was her first boyfriend and perhaps the inspiration for *Magia* (or at least that's what he thinks).

At fifteen, Óscar Pardo was two years older than she was. According to Colombian reporters, Óscar was completely in love with Shakira and had to woo her for two months before he finally got her to say yes. The moment of acceptance was sealed with a kiss, the singer's first. From that day on they were always together at parties and at the beach. They would go out dancing, to dinner, or to play volleyball. They lived with the lightness that only two teenagers in love have. She would play the guitar and he would listen….He says she confided in him her dream of becoming a professional singer.

Even though the relationship ended the following year, the singer still remembers Óscar affectionately. So affectionately, in fact, that whenever she goes back to Barranquilla, she stops by his house to visit.

THE MAGIC HAS JUST BEGUN

With the vibrant energy and fresh dreams of a thirteen-year-old, *Magia* was born. By the time the record was launched, Shakira was fourteen, with kinky hair and the body of a child. Although the record didn't sell well—according to Colombian reporters the record sold less than a thousand copies—the experience of making it was valuable for myriad reasons. In the first place it allowed the artist to enter the hidden underworld of making an album, a complicated and chauvinistic universe with its own laws. Recording an album is not the same as composing songs, and Shakira had the chance to learn that at an early age. As the artist would later recall when asked if she ever felt discriminated against as a woman: "Yes, but not just for being a woman, but also because of my age. At one point in my life both these factors joined and became an obstacle for me. If you run across a thirteen-year-old girl who is 5'2" , who is opinionated and wants to be solely in charge of the production of her own record, and if you find an executive in a suit and tie, who's around forty and has worked for the company for ten years…"

Magia was released in June 1991. It was launched in the Teatro Amira de la Rosa, the biggest theater in Barranquilla, to a full house, before an audience of about eight hundred people says César Navarro. There was print, radio, and television coverage. Far from being nervous or anxious, the dancer confirms that Shakira was happy, rejoicing, and radiant. She was in the best of moods and her positive energy flooded the stage. She had worked so hard and so meticulously that one couldn't imagine anything going wrong. And indeed everything went as planned: the choreography, the voices, and the costumes…the debut was a success. As she often did, Shakira wore boots, and a black and gold outfit with sequins. Skinny and with her kinky hair, she moved freely across the stage and danced alongside her band mates like the small "diva" that she was.

They performed a similar show in cities along the Atlantic coast such as Cartagena, Santa Marta, and Riohacha, and other cities in the interior such as Medellín, Cali, and Bogotá, among others. They traveled through different towns and performed at various events, festivals, and theaters.

Like the professionals they were, before every show Shakira and her dancers would review the choreography and the sound. Even when they weren't performing, they would get together with the choreographers and rehearse practically every day. Shakira was already demonstrating her obsessiveness about her moves, which she would rehearse over and over tirelessly. And she did the same with her songs.

According to César Navarro, working with Shakira was fun and relaxing. It was easy to be with her, not only on stage but also off. She talked with everyone to make sure they were happy and that they had what they needed. If she detected even the smallest distress, she asked about it, listened, and gave advice. "She is like that, she feels others' problems as if they're her own." He remembers her as a very sensitive person and full of positive energy. "She was a tireless worker, but more than anything, performing was a total blast," he said.

In these first performances as a professional, her preparation was not just physical; before every show she took a couple of minutes and in silence, with her eyes closed, she meditated and prayed. It was part of her routine. First they would go over the program, then they would warm up their voices, then Shakira would retire to her dressing room or find a spot on the side of the stage and would begin to pray with her eyes closed. She asked her dancers to pray with her many times. "You too, pray, pray," she would tell them as they purposely looked away, trying to make her think that they were distracted by something else, all the while smiling at her suggestion. Everyone in the group prepared behind the scenes in his or her own way, and this was the way Shakira had found to fill herself with energy and communicate with God. Once on stage, everything was magic.

In addition to the video to the song "Magia," which appeared on music programs in Colombia and Venezuela, Shakira and her dancers recorded a promotional video for Santa Marta, a tourist resort, that was called "Esta noche voy contigo a bailar," and that played on regional flights.

Despite the weak sales of the album, Shakira's shows with her dancers almost always sold out and the audience invariably ended up dancing in the aisles. More than once they drove the audience wild, literally. For example, while performing the principle number in Riohacha in an interschools festival, Shakira, Nidia, and the dancers ended the show running down the halls of the school trying to escape fans who wanted to hug and kiss them. As César Navarro remembers, after running for half an hour, they had to lock themselves in a classroom, but the crowd was so unruly that the girls ended up breaking down the door. It was quite a scare: due to the suffocating heat, Nidia ended up fainting inside the classroom. Shakira tried to help her, but there was not much she could do.

Finally, the police arrived and Shakira, Nidia, and the dancers were able to leave the school, scratched and bitten, but intact thanks to the police.

Something similar happened at a show in Maicao, where the stage was accessible to the audience. A man went up to Shakira and gave her flowers and a kiss. Later another man, this one drunk, started hugging Shakira and refused to let go. She became very frightened. She couldn't even bring the microphone to her mouth because her arm was stuck under the blubbering man's arm. The dancers had to intervene to save the petite singer from the arms of that fan and many others that had joined him. In the end the situation got so out of control that they had to retreat to their dressing rooms and were unable to finish the show.

At this point, Shakira was recognized wherever she performed and the audience knew who she was and knew her songs. *Magia* proved to be her ticket into the music world, even if it was only a small one for the time being. Among other things, she stood out on the radio and on television because there weren't that many teens in her country doing the kind of dance pop that she was doing. Almost all the pop music at the time came from foreign soloists and groups, mainly from the United States.

Thanks to this first record Shakira was invited to the Festival de la Canción in Buga, in 1991, and participated in the show for the Elección de la Niña Bolívar in Cartagena, in 1992. Among her first international festivals, that year she also participated in the Festival de la Independencia Cubana in Miami.

Also thanks to *Magia*, Shakira won her first important awards: the Premio Cantante Revelación of Barranquilla in 1991, and the Premio Superestrella de Oro the following year.

SWEET FIFTEEN

In Latin America, when a girl turns fifteen, she ceases to be a child and becomes a young woman. The tradition is to celebrate that birthday with a big party. Among other things, there is a cake, the birthday girl dresses in white, and at a certain point she waltzes with her father....Well, Shakira didn't have all of that, but she did have a party that was made to order.

Compared to all the pomp and circumstance associated with *quinceañeras*, Shakira's was modest. On February 2, 1992, Nidia and William rented out a hall in a hotel in Barranquilla and invited all of Shakira's friends, including people from the industry. Some of the people who joined the festivities were her promoter, her choreographer, and her dancers, who at that time were like family. She did not dress in white. Instead she was dressed radiantly and elegantly but also comfortably enough to dance and enjoy the party like any other guest.

Only one year after the launch of *Magia*, Shakira got the best gift a fifteen-year-old could receive, even though it wasn't exactly on her birthday. A jury from her country selected her to represent Colombia in the OTI (Organización de la Televisión Iberoamericana) Festival de la Canción. This festival presents one representative from each Spanish-speaking country to compete with one song each. The jury is composed of recognized artists and people from the industry, and the festival tends to be a sample of new talent that will go on to gain international recognition.

But Shakira never attended the festival, which that year was held in Spain. When the time came to fill out the application, the singer had not yet turned sixteen, the minimum age required to participate. That did not diminish the honor conferred to her by her country.

Uncertainty, the Worst Danger

If the first fifteen years of Shakira's life gave her a taste of how sweet stardom could be, the next one would show her that the road of the artist was not an easy one. A year and a half after releasing her first record, she needed to start the production of her second, a project for which Sony Colombia had higher expectations. Though *Magia* wasn't much of a hit in the sales department, it was frequently played on local radio stations and had demonstrated the singer's potential.

For a teenager who had tasted the power of the stage and had learned how to lead a group of dancers, the experience of returning to the recording studio was disastrous. Her artistic independence no longer existed. She was no longer at the helm, and there was no audience shouting out their approval. Indeed, it was the exact opposite.

The decision to come out with a new album at that time was not Shakira's, but the record label's. To Sony it was important to create new songs, especially a hit, that would increase the small following she was already enjoying. The production of this second album, this time produced by Eduardo Paz, was perhaps one of the most frustrating experiences in Shakira's career.

After several hard months spent in the recording studio and the mixing room, after coming up with ideas that never quite worked for Shakira, the final product was an odd album, with eight songs that did not sit well with the artist. Sony Colombia, apparently satisfied with the record, described it in the press release as "a spectacular album, with a very North American ballad treatment." It went on to say that it had "profound and direct lyrics, filled with magic and poetry, and a search for new sounds mixing rock guitars, acoustic pianos, and a saxophone style not unlike Kenny G's." This second album included songs from both Shakira and other composers, including a song written by Eddie Sierra, who wrote "El amor de mi vida," one of the songs on Ricky Martin's first solo album. The publicists singled out the song "1968," in which Shakira "analyzes what occurred during the spring of Woodstock, the hippies and the events that shook the world twenty-five years ago." But Shakira was not pleased. As a matter of fact, she was so dissatisfied with the album that she decided not to promote it, according to TV y Novelas.

Ironically, the record was titled Peligro (Danger) and it put her career in jeopardy. Not only had her first record not reached the sales figures expected, but now the second one wouldn't even have Shakira's support. The result? The rehearsals and live performances were canceled. No more videos, no more sequined outfits. Instead, what was left was the bitter taste of a record that died soon after it was born.

Even though the artist did not support Peligro live, and according to TV y Novelas, might have asked Sony not to promote it either, the record company did send it to a few radio stations, and after several months, the song "Tú serás la historia de mi vida" was still playing on some local stations. But beyond that, the record would go down in history with very little glory and fewer than a thousand copies sold.

"I accept challenges without looking back," Shakira said years later. And nothing proves this philosophy more than the way she managed her career during those difficult times, when in the beginning of

1993 her popularity was not yet her ace in the hole. That same year, before the not so loved *Peligro* came into the world, the artist was invited to participate in one of the most popular contests in Latin America, the Festival de la Canción de Viña del Mar. Celebrated each year in the small coastal town in the north of Chile, the festival serves as a launching pad for new Hispanic and Portuguese singers. It's worth noting that there is supposedly a curse that haunts this festival. Legend has it that those who have won this contest have very short careers that end after their first record.

Shakira arrived in Viña del Mar in February of 1993 to compete with "Eres," a song on the album *Peligro*. That windy southern summer night, the young but confident Colombian sang in Chile in front of television cameras that broadcast her image across the entire continent. Under that star-filled night, she dazzled the audience with her voice and convinced the jury that her talent would take her far: when the contest was over she took home third prize. She had triumphed in Viña del Mar; she had avoided the curse of first place and had come out victorious with one of her own songs. And as if that weren't enough, she was named Queen of the Festival. All in one day.

Among the judges was a young talent named Ricky Martin, who at that time was only twenty years old, and who, moved by the voice of the young Colombian, voted her as his favorite.

The following day Shakira flew home with the satisfaction of having won a decisive battle. As proof, she had the first major international trophy of her career: a splendid silver Seagull. Happily and probably with a certain taste of revenge, Shakira once again rubbed her recognition in the face of all those who dared to doubt her. As in years before, she had had to go outside her circle for her talent to be recognized. And as in the past, that small circle would later be at her feet.

3

MAKING ALLIES

"One door closes, another one opens." —Shakira
during a concert

When Shakira landed in Bogotá in February 1993, coming from Santiago, Chile, with her silver-plated Seagull in her arms, very few people knew who the young, smiling, long black haired girl was or why so many journalists were waiting for her. It may have been because this one was the most significant award in her short career, the one that established her as one of the most promising singers in Colombia.

But that year, few would see her on stage. Shakira decided to take a break that would keep her away from the entertainment world for about a year. She took refuge in school, focusing on graduating from high school and then figuring out what she would do with her career. After all, the trophy could not reverse the sour taste of the artistic failure of *Peligro*. She had to think carefully about her next step in the industry, since her next record could easily be her last.

She began the school year completely focused on her studies to get her diploma as soon as possible. It was her senior year, and since school was never a problem for our artist, it didn't take her long to reach her goal. By December of that year, without a hitch, the singer received her diploma and was free to think exclusively about her artistic goals. No one could prevent her from going after her dreams, which in essence had not changed a bit: she would become a famous singer. And those who were around her at that time already knew she would make it.

In addition to her studies, Shakira had free time to spend with her friends, go to the beach, and play volleyball. It was during one of those games that she met the second person who would steal her heart. Like her neighbor, this new love was also named Óscar and was older than she was.

Óscar Ulloa and Shakira met when she was finishing high school and he was already a college student. He is reported to have been captivated by her beauty and was brave enough to let her know. Very much a gentleman, he invited her on a date, and Shakira did not hesitate to accept. She gave him her number and waited for him to call…but he made her wait. And that may have intrigued Shakira even more. He called a couple of days later, they went out to eat, he declared his feelings for her, and she reciprocated. The romance that began in Barranquilla would continue in Bogotá, where Shakira was headed to conquer her dream and where Óscar would continue his studies.

PERSISTENCE: HER FIRST ALLY

"When I wake up, my first thought is that they should let me sleep for five minutes. That's all I think about, five more minutes."

When Shakira finished high school, many people around her, including her promoters and the executives at Sony, insisted that she had to be in Bogotá, the epicenter of the music world in Colombia.

Even though Shakira would be sad to leave her city, her home, and her people, she understood that she had to move if she wanted to succeed.

She had outgrown Barranquilla; it was too small for her dreams of stardom. She sensed that destiny had something big in store for her, and she knew it wasn't in a house cooking and taking care of children. As soon as she got her hands on that highly anticipated diploma, she packed her bags and moved with her mother to Bogotá.

Nidia and her daughter arrived in the capital and rented a small room at a university boardinghouse. The first thing they did was to go to Sony's headquarters to inform them of their new address and to put themselves at their disposal. The second thing was to seek out press. They did everything they could to get Shakira mentioned in newspaper or magazine articles, no matter how small the item. The third thing Shakira did was enroll in a gym…being in the capital without a job was not going to prevent her from getting the exercise she had grown up with.

After she had called to introduce herself to a couple of entertainment outlets, the magazine *TV Guía*, later renamed *TV y Novelas*, interviewed the singer. That was a small but significant achievement, not because of the article that would later appear, but because of the relationship that developed between the singer and the magazine. Shakira, whom the publisher, Omaira Ríos, already knew thanks to her triumph in Viña del Mar the year before, impressed her to such an extent that she recommended her as a client to her friend María del Rosario Sánchez, a journalist who had recently arrived in Bogotá and, like Shakira, was making her way in the city. Sánchez became Shakira's first press agent.

"We knocked on a lot of doors in the industry. We would pray for fifteen days for at least a short segment of ten seconds on television, or an article of five lines in the paper. But she had all the discipline in the world, and she knew what she wanted," recalls Sánchez, who advised Shakira on her image and P.R. for almost two years.

Those first few months in Bogotá were all about moving and learning for Shakira, on an emotional and professional level. She was alone in a big city where the only familiar face was her mother's. She'd left behind her father, her school friends, the kids from the neighborhood, the dancers, the beach...now she was living in an environment with an entirely different conception of time and life.

Like a good Barranquillera, Shakira began to adapt, without losing her sense of humor or getting discouraged, and always keeping her objective in sight. And as often occurs for this persistent artist, good luck didn't take long to tap her on the shoulder. A short time after her first interview appeared, about half a year after coming to Bogotá, she got a call from the producers of a new soap opera that was to be produced by Cempro Televisión, a former large production company. The screen test was quick, and a couple of days later Shakira was signing her first contract in the city, not as a singer, but as an actress. But not just any actress: she landed the lead role for the new soap opera *El Oasis*, where she would play the rich girl hopelessly in love with the wrong man. Not a bad beginning.

This first job was like manna from heaven. It meant the end of monetary problems, and she and her mother could now rent a larger apartment. But her heart, her passion, and her mind were still dedicated to her music. According to María del Rosario Sánchez, Shakira lived for her songs, from the moment she woke up to the time she fell asleep. She took singing classes and voice training and learned breathing techniques and how to play the flute. During her free time she wrote lyrics or made up melodies.

She would be so focused on her music that sometimes at two in the morning she would still be up writing lyrics, even though she had to be up early to tape the episodes of the show. Waking her up in the morning was one of the most difficult tasks in the world. Sánchez still remembers the great "wars" she had trying to wake Shakira up. "Waking her up was impossible, no one could get her out of that bed," she said.

Television: The Unexpected Ally

In *El Oasis*, which aired Monday through Friday, Shakira played Luisa María Rico, a modest, noble girl from a well-to-do family, hopelessly in love with the wrong man. Like a Shakespearean tragedy, Luisa María and Salomón Perdigón (Pedro Rendón) loved each other intensely, but their fathers, who were twin brothers, had hated each other ever since her father took sole control of the family fortune, leaving his brother in dire poverty. Against all odds, Luisa María and Salomón prove that love is stronger than all the hate in the world and end up getting married.

The soap opera did not get high ratings, but it was enough to put Shakira's image in the homes of hundreds of thousands of people who followed the adventures of Luisa María and Salomón. Shakira took advantage of her lead role and started accepting invitations to various events and functions. She also rode the TV role onto the pages of a lot of fashion magazines

Even though during the months of the soap's taping Shakira stayed far from the music scene, she never stopped writing. And she did not write only at night. The set was four or five hours outside Bogotá, practically in the middle of the desert—an ideal place to retreat and find inspiration. That was exactly what the young poet would do when she managed to escape. One of her fellow cast members, the actress Xilena Sicardi, remembers that during her breaks Shakira would disappear. She withdrew from the noise in order to write in peace. "She was always thinking about composing some song or fixing another one she'd already written," Xilena told *TV y Novelas*.

Another thing to which Shakira was devoted was reading, and not just the script for the day's shoot. On every trip she took along a book, sometimes self-help and personal growth; other times, a work of Latin American literature, which at that time were her favorites. As for music, Nirvana was a constant for the young artist.

But her television adventure was short. Her life on the small screen ended with the last episode of *El Oasis*. After a year of studying lines and taping scenes, Shakira decided to kill her acting career abruptly. She had tasted what it meant to be an actress and to work in TV. She had learned how to give fake kisses, to cry for an unrequited love, even to marry. Though she was not fond of the kissing scenes, Shakira was a professional and fulfilled her role. But at the moment of truth, her desire to sing and compose was greater than the security of a good salary at the end of the month.

El Oasis had allowed her to widen her network of contacts and create a buzz. In that year she met a lot of people in the entertainment industry and, especially important, in television, the medium that would become a great ally on her road to fame. It was during this time that she met Patricia Téllez, who was then the Director of Special Projects for Caracol Television, the only private channel in Colombia, and the one with the highest artistic quality. Caracol Television also belonged to one of the most powerful financial cartels in Colombia, the Grupo Santodomingo. Through Téllez, Shakira became the channel's exclusive artist.

By the end of 1994, those who had never heard Shakira sing before, now knew her name and recognized her face at least. And for a pop singer, that is half the battle.

HER DIET: AN ALLY LATE IN COMING

"I wouldn't change a thing on my body; everything I have, my legs, my hips, my fingers, even my pinkie toe and my badly manicured nails, has been with me for a long time."

If you asked her, Shakira never had a problem with her physique. As a child she was always slim and athletic, and when it was time to dance she had total control of her body. However, during that first year of chasing the press in Bogotá, Shakira was faced with something totally new to her: the need to please magazine editors, who wanted to see her thinner.

Confronting the obsession that magazines have with anorexic bodies was not easy. One of Shakira's biggest weaknesses was chocolate, especially candy bars. Her craving was so great that her press agent had to make a deal with her: she could have her chocolate every day, but only the amount that Sánchez gave her, and no more. Her addiction to chocolate became the second reason for "wars" with her press agent. These "wars," it's worth noting, were never aggressive; there was no shrieking, or even harsh words. But for Sánchez, it really was a headache to try to make Shakira understand that if she wanted a career in entertainment she had to watch her figure every day.

Many in the press commented on how chubby Shakira had gotten, Sánchez remembers. Shakira surely heard it too. But how could she change her eating habits and forsake her diet of fried, greasy, and spicy food? One of Shakira's greatest pleasures was eating as she herself said. Among her favorite dishes were shell fish, fried plantains, and Arabic food, all full of fat. She also loved soda. "She could drink a whole liter of Coca Cola with ice," recalls Sánchez. To make the issue of dieting even more challenging, Don William disagreed with the magazines and thought his daughter was "too skinny" and would give her vitamins, which exasperated Sánchez, who thought Shakira did not need them.

In the height of her adolescence, with so many changes in her life, Shakira had to face one more change in her routine: her diet. But she never lost sleep over dieting. Instead of taking drastic measures, which so many adolescent girls unfortunately do, Shakira made some key changes to her diet, and with that she was satisfied. According to her ex–press agent, the artist decreased the amount of wheat and chocolate she ate, and stopped drinking soda entirely. Those small changes in her eating habits made a substantial change in her image, leaving her face better defined and her waist smaller. In the meantime, she never stopped going to the gym, so burning calories and maintaining a toned body was not a difficult task.

Six years later, Shakira continues to learn about nutrition and above all she has learned to listen to her body. Referring to her eating habits she said, "I don't do diets, but after five o'clock I don't eat any type of bread. I finally learned that after that time of day my metabolism slows down."

In addition to improving her physique, her small foray into the small screen resulted in another prize…although not exactly one she'd been pursuing. In 1994 the new magazine *TV y Novelas* had decided to celebrate its first anniversary with a contest for the Best Backside in Television. Basically, it was a competition between the rear ends of celebrities in television, and they asked Shakira to participate. Even though many advised her not to do it, Sánchez thought it would be a good way for Shakira to get press. Shakira agreed, with the sole condition that she would not be photographed in a bikini, but so that readers could see her body and be encouraged to vote for her, she did agree to wear shorts. Shakira's attractive body took her to the finals along with a professional model. The readers of the magazine ended up voting Shakira's derriere the winner. At that point she had no choice but to be photographed in a bikini, for the cover. For a woman as shy as Shakira, who doesn't even feel comfortable changing in front of strangers during a photo session, these photos were an assault on her privacy. In the end at the awards ceremony Shakira was presented with a trophy…for her derriere!

The editors of *TV y Novelas* thought the contest helped Shakira get more attention, but for the artist it was degrading. As she later recognized, "The magazine included me and at the time I really couldn't complain because I thought I should just be grateful. Now that I reflect on it, I think I went over the top. I'm not proud to have been a participant. I think it was part of my learning process, and I know that nothing like that will ever happen again."

Once again, as with the music teacher when she was a child, her trust in herself and her faith in her dreams saved her. Shakira always knew that in addition to a nice butt, she also had a good head on her shoulders, good instincts, and an exceptional voice that she could count on. Thanks to her business savvy she knew how to find the right people to support her career. She had managed to get interviews in fan magazines and as a result had landed her first television offer. She had made the most of her short acting career and gained the respect of Patricia Téllez, who a year later would become not only a great friend but also her manager and consultant.

Shakira proved that when it came to recognizing allies, her instinct did not fail her. That first year in Bogotá she also met the man who would take her to stardom. And once again, her instinct was not wrong.

Luis Fernando Ochoa: Creative Ally

While Shakira was developing her acting career she could see more clearly every day that her true calling was songwriting and singing. She wanted it so badly that it was only a matter of time before she found the key to her most desired goal. When Sony Discos picked her to participate in a compilation album with various artists called *Nuestro rock*, Shakira must have jumped for joy. This was her opportunity to show everyone what her music really was and what she could do with her voice, beyond repeating the lines of a script. Now all she had to do was compose the song, since otherwise the record label would use one of her old ones, probably from *Peligro*.

While she was sitting on the bus on the way home from taping the soap, in the middle of nowhere, the lyrics to "Dónde estás corazón?" passed through her mind. The inspiration vanished, but the methodical artist had jotted down the phrases and ideas on a piece of paper. Luckily.

When the time came to add the music to those lyrics, Shakira met with Luis Fernando Ochoa, a producer that Sony had contracted for this record, who, in addition to being a musician, composed jingles for television. He was in charge of helping Shakira with the music for her song, and he did the same for three other artists who participated in the album *Nuestro rock*.

The chemistry born between the singer and the producer was like dynamite. And when it came time to create "Dónde estás corazón?" it exploded. She brought the lyrics and he added the music. They worked together on some arrangements, and a couple of days later they entered the recording studio. The process was simple, fun, and creative. Shakira had found a producer who would listen to and understand her, someone with whom creating a song was a pleasure, not torture. It had cost her *Peligro* but here she was, finally in front of the producer she needed.

To add more magic to this story, "Dónde estás corazón?" was a hit on radio stations all over the country. In fact, it was the only hit from the entire compilation *Nuestro rock,* and this achievement was a credit to the Mebarak-Ochoa team. Radio stations played the song almost incessantly, and in a couple of weeks all of Columbia was singing along.

That song saved her. As the artist knew all too well, her name had been on the Sony Discos blacklist. Her last album had been a failure, and it had been more than a year since she had done anything. And if the third album wasn't successful, it would be the end of her career. "Dónde estás corazón?" was her salvation, the hit that revived her career.

Luis Fernando Ochoa was already a recognized musician in Bogotá. His career included commercial jingles and soundtracks for television programs. He had worked for Sony as an artistic producer on various occasions, and he was, and is, highly respected within the company. Besides his musical talents, "Luisfer" is intuitive and practical, a good combination in this industry. He was the one who saw Shakira's potential beyond the image of a sweet balladeer, a potential that the record label couldn't see.

After over a year in which Shakira had walked in shadows, the light at the end of the tunnel was finally apparent. Slowly, her road was becoming clear and she could see beyond the present.

PIES DESCALZOS

"*I've always had a hidden tendency
to go against the masses.*"

The success of "Dónde estás corazón?" was not just Sony's. Going into her third album, the record company had to renegotiate her contract. Now a matured Shakira, knowledgeable about the business and with more ammunition, demanded a contract that gave her everything she needed to make the music she wanted. According to a former promoter of hers, among other things she demanded more authority over her repertoire, her lyrics and arrangements, and asked for all her videos to have film quality.

Shakira had proved that she could make a hit, and Sony ended up giving its artist more power. This time the singer would not have the record company breathing down her neck, perhaps to the credit of Ochoa, who could finish a record in two months. Instead of submitting to the demands of the record company, this time Shakira was able to take her time and channel all her dreams, thoughts, and images into her music.

our years had passed since her first record, and she was no longer that little girl with legs like "two sticks with kneecaps," as she described herself, bewitched by the microphone. She was eighteen years old and had traveled far, and along the way she had picked up the third-place prize at the Festival de Viña del Mar, a hit playing nonstop on the radio, and the leading role in a daily soap that broadcast her image throughout Colombia. She had taken advantage of her acting career to do interviews and to appear in several women's magazines, even if only to demonstrate exercises for the legs or the rear end. She was also able to take care of herself financially; she had enough income now to move from the boardinghouse to a nice apartment in the outskirts of Bogotá, an apartment she would later buy.

Spiritually, Shakira had not changed. She continued to go to mass on Sundays and to pray. She regularly visited hospitalized AIDS patients, talking with and sometimes singing to them. Every time she got on stage she continued to pray to God, whose blessing she asked, offering up her work as a tribute. As for her fears, she became afraid of death and was uncomfortable talking about it. It even became impossible for her to go to funerals, especially after a cousin with whom she was very close died and left the artist with great emptiness in her heart.

Professionally, Shakira was growing by giant leaps. And those who attended the awards show of *TV y Novelas* in Bogotá toward the end of 1994 were witnesses to the change. Sánchez was able to get Shakira a spot in the concert where originally only Alejandra Guzmán and Paulina Rubio were going to sing. Whereas these two artists, already celebrated by the public, sang on stage and did their acts with fabulous choreography, Shakira sang three songs with no choreography and no backup dancers, which stunned everyone. Artists and journalists alike could not stop talking about her progress; with her presence and her voice alone, she had overshadowed the honored singers.

On the eve of her third album Shakira was growing up and was becoming a much more knowledgeable woman, independent and sure of herself. In one interview Shakira put it this way: "I think that if I hadn't had the failure of *Peligro*, I wouldn't have woken up and found the determination to stop what I was doing and reevaluate my objectives. In other words, if the soles of my feet didn't hurt I wouldn't have noticed that my shoes were too small. If I hadn't hit that wall, I would not have come out barefoot, and revealed myself exactly as I am."

As she had done literally on the main avenue of Bogotá, the petite poet took off her shoes and began to walk barefoot. Stripping herself of everything but her dreams, Shakira began to work on her ideas, based on old experiences, on situations that grabbed her attention, and on themes that obsessed her. In the shower, in a cab, in bed, every time a sentence or an idea emerged, the obsessed teen would drop everything and run in search of pen and paper. She rewrote new and old songs and composed new melodies...always with the help of her new ally, Luis Fernando Ochoa.

During rehearsal, Shakira would go to Ochoa's studio with her lyrics, old or new, to rework them with Luis Fernando, who also composed a great deal of the music, and who was in charge of the artistic production. There was no outline; it was more a flow of ideas, a collaborative work that allowed Shakira to find her voice in front of a microphone. After a couple of months of preproduction, trying to figure out the content of the album and recording demos in the studio, Shakira entered the recording studios in February of 1995.

Pies descalzos, Dreams Come True

"*Pies descalzos* comes from my need to express a certain nonconformity I have toward norms, toward rules, toward all social conventions," Shakira said in 1996.

Between February and July of the previous year, Shakira had hardly seen the light of day. During those months, she was in recording studios mixing the songs she had written the year before, splitting her time between the studios in Bogotá and Miami, Sonido Azulado and Ocean V.U., respectively. With the help of a few special guests and the musical coordination of Luis Fernando Ochoa, a record that combined rock, ballads, and pop, with a speck of reggae and a little disco, emerged.

It is said that the third time is the charm. And in this case the saying could not be more precise. Like a musical rebirth, Shakira created what would later be called her masterpiece, the milestone that divided her career into a "before" and "after." With *Pies descalzos* Shakira achieved every artist's dream: a record with a voice of its own, a collection of songs in which she could see herself. As she has said: "I think I achieved my signature, from the cover to the last vocal of the last song."

On *Pies descalzos* Shakira began to demonstrate the vocal play that would become her signature in the years ahead. Her vibrato voice, still young, now had much more nuance and body than on previous records. The passage of time had improved her poems, and her songs now truly evoked an atmosphere.

But if over the previous few years Shakira's voice and ideas had grown notably, the budget for her new album had not. For the production of *Pies descalzos* Sony gave her a total of $100,000 since the sales estimate was not over 100,000 copies, according to *TV y Novelas* in its Shakira special issue. Indeed, instead of launching the album in the Teatro El Nogal, a modern theater where almost every record of some importance is released, Sony reserved the Teatro Nacional La Castellana, a more quaint venue with a much smaller capacity. It was definitely an austere presentation, with no banquet or fanfare, no "hanger" for the press, and no VIPs. Many of those who attended the launch of *Pies descalzos* went because someone happened to invite them or they heard about it, or because, in fact, there was some sort of buzz about this new album. But the buzz wasn't coming from Sony, it was coming from the press.

As Shakira would later recall, "*Pies descalzos* didn't get major support at the beginning, but the album began to gain it little by little." Her comparison: "It was like those beauty queens who do not have the biggest supporters but in the end win the crown."

Behind the group of journalists and curious onlookers who had gathered that night, the television cameras of Caracol began to roll. Whether mobile or still, the cameras caught the entire concert for the only station allowed to broadcast her. That night cameras and onlookers could see an artist standing tall on stage. Her sensational stage presence found support, this time, in the strength of her voice and in the freshness and intelligence of her songs. *Magia* and *Peligro* were behind her, forever. This artist had made a 180-degree turn, and those who knew her could not stop admiring the radical change in her voice, her songs, and her attitude.

Shakira was reborn; she had gone through a "metamorphosis," as she likes to say. Her attitude was that of an honest balladeer who likes to express her dreams and frustrations in her songs, whether pop, rock, or reggae. She had eradicated the superfluous in order to stay with the authentic. That is why it made sense that in the middle of her concert she would take off her shoes and sing the title track of her album, *Pies descalzos*, barefoot.

Nothing was left of that kinky-haired little girl trying to be an adult with thick makeup and sequined dresses. In her place stood a complex woman, wearing pants and armed with an acoustic guitar. There was no longer taped background music; in its place were musicians of flesh and blood, as she wanted. On October 6, 1995, Shakira launched *Pies descalzos* in the Colombian capital and took a historic step forward in the world of music. that night Shakira took the wheel and started steering her career. At last she was the captain of her own destiny, even if it was only her artistic destiny.

Even though there was very little promotion for *Pies descalzos* before launch, the day after, several critics in different media were talking. Not all the reviews were favorable. One journalist for *TV y Novelas* reported that as soon as the concert was over, one group of critics came out alleging that certain themes came straight from the London group The Pretenders. This reporter recalls that the following day the number of critics making the same comparisons multiplied, and Shakira was deeply hurt. She did not expect it. Shakira even had to endure a radio interview with a journalist who was trying to prove by any means necessary that the artist had borrowed part of her music. For those who already felt some sympathy toward Shakira, this was one of the lowest blows. However, neither The Pretenders nor their record label ever voiced concern, turning these criticisms into something of a controversy, but nothing more. After several days, the whole scandal was thrown aside and the accusations forgotten.

But beyond this bitter episode, the majority of those who attended the concert that night left greatly satisfied, surprised, and awed by the new talent developing before their eyes.

GOD: THAT ETERNAL ALLY

"When I was finishing *Pies descalzos* I got on my knees and prayed to God: grant me this wish, I just need to sell a million copies, that's all! The story goes that I promised Him something, and the trouble is now I don't remember what," said Shakira a year later.

As evidenced by this anecdote, it is not rare to hear the artist talking about God, so no one is surprised that she would have asked for such a miracle (or that He would grant it). What is curious is finding a rocker/balladeer who reveals so openly and emphatically her devotion to the Catholic religion. For her it is not about organized religion or dogma—attending mass or confessing her sins to the priest. It's more a way of being, a spiritual lifestyle, as though she internalized the idea of God she learned in school among the missionary nuns.

Unlike many singers, who are raised Catholic and then grow up and turn their backs on Catholicism because they consider it rigid or somehow inadequate, Shakira sees her religion as a secure and essential bridge, like a way of understanding that allows her to see beyond daily reality.

Shakira explains: "My religious education reinforced my restlessness about all things spiritual and made me start to think about my actions." To her, God is the creator of the universe, and also the creator of her music, or better said, the generator of her songs. In this context, Shakira is something like a medium or an angel, a messenger and instrument of divine inspiration. Sometimes, she has said, she has found her own words to be foreign, to the point that she has had to reread what she wrote in order to understand it. "I love to feel that dependence, that connection with God. It is what keeps my hands and my mouth fertile. And I know that if my relationship with God were to change, if one day I were to distance myself from Him, I would surely dry up."

Perhaps it is because of Shakira's devotion to her religion, that God and the Bible are present in many of her lyrics: "Tú mordiste la manzana y renunciastes al paraíso ..." (You took a bite of the apple and gave up paradise); "Fuiste polvo y polvo eres..." (Dust thou art, and into dust thou shalt return). And sharing her ideas of the Church, the song "Se quiere...se mata" emerged. But nothing about her lyrics could categorize her as a Christian singer: her songs do not contain messages of salvation, nor is her mission to illuminate divine truths. It is just that to Shakira God is present in reality, in the people, ideas, and situations that surround her.

Perhaps also related to her spiritual search, or maybe because all artists resist the limitations of time, time is another obsession for Shakira. Her lyrics are filled with allusions to time, past and future, or on the other hand, deliberately atemporal moments. "Mil años no me alcanzarán para borrarte y olvidar" (A thousand years isn't enough to forget you); "Y aprendí a quitarle al tiempo los segundos…" (And I learned to take the seconds away from time); "y retumba en mis oídos el tic-tac de los relojes…" (and the ticking of the clocks echoes in my ears).

In her daily life, Shakira admits that she is always late and lives in a constant battle with wristwatches, which she prefers not to wear. "Time and I are not good friends," she concluded in one interview.

THE MUSES

"Because of my lyrics, anyone would think that I live a mortified reality, but look, my veins are in perfect condition. They don't abandon me every day."

If God and time permeate the creations of the artist, there are other, more terrestrial sources that also nourish her music. According to what Shakira told the press when she was in Mexico on her *Pies descalzos* tour, that year she had been listening to a lot of acoustic rock. Among the musicians and groups she mentioned as her favorites were many very different artists: Tom Petty, R.E.M., Nirvana, Silvio Rodríguez, The Police, The Cure, Soda Stereo, and Mecano. They and others surely influenced the music she wanted to create: a powerful ballad, a passionate song with rough edges.

At the moment of writing, however, Shakira's poetry had more to do with her failed loves than with glamorizing any dark spiritual chasm. This artist who is sensitive to everyday reality—her own and that of others—says: "I write about what's on my mind, what I wonder about, what causes me to doubt, what makes me uncomfortable…my stories, or other people's stories that catch my attention and motivate me to speak."

Shakira at the 1999 Alma Awards in Pasadena, California. *Fitzroy Barrett/Globe Photos*

Shakira arrives at the Billboard Latin Music Awards on April 22, 1999, held at the Fontainebleau Hotel in Miami Beach. Shakira won for Best Pop Album. *AFP/Corbis*

Shakira is escorted into the James L. Knight Center in downtown Miami for the 1999 Univisión Gala Lo Nuestro. *Associated Press/Miami Herald*

In July 1999 Shakira (center) had to be protected by bodyguards and police officers at La Gran Discoteca record store in San Juan, Puerto Rico. Approximately 1,000 fans mobbed the store to get autographs. *AP/Wide World Photos*

Shakira dances on stage during a concert given before an audience of 40,000 people in a polo field in Buenos Aires, Argentina, in May of 2000. Shakira had given a series of concerts in Buenos Aires one month earlier, and she returned by popular demand. *Reuters/ Corbis*

Latin music celebrities (left to right) producer Emilio Estefan Jr. and singers Jon Secada, Shakira, and José Feliciano perform the finale at the First Latin Academy of Recording Arts & Sciences "Person of the Year" tribute dinner and concert. Estefan, who is considered the "godfather of Latin pop," was honored with the award. September 11, 2000, Beverly Hills. *Reuters/Corbis*

Shakira performs at the First Annual Latin Grammy Awards at the Staples Center in Los Angeles on September 13, 2000. Shakira stole the show and took home two Grammys. *AFP/Corbis*

Shakira and her boyfriend, Antonio de la Rúa, in Punta del Este, Uruguay, on September 28, 2000.
Reuters/Corbis

Shakira holds her two Grammys, one for Best Female Pop Vocal Performance and the other for Best Female Rock Vocal Performance, at the First Annual Latin Grammy Awards at the Staples Center in Los Angeles.
AFP/Corbis

Shakira waves to fans in a Guatemala City hotel. April 17, 2000. *AP/Wide World Photos*

Shakira hugs fans at the Uruguayan seaside resort of Punta del Este, where she spent several months writing songs for her new album. October 29, 2000. *Reuters/ Corbis*

Dressed like a golden mermaid, Shakira received her first Grammy award on February 21, 2001. She won for Best Latin Pop Album for *MTV Unplugged*. *AFP/Corbis*

And what caught Shakira's attention between the ages of sixteen and eighteen? A variety of things. For example, "Estoy aquí" was inspired by the story of a friend who was depressed because his girlfriend had broken up with him; he had confessed to Shakira that he deeply regretted certain things he had done and that he would do anything to get her back. These are the simple stories that moved her and motivated her writing.

She was also moved by the profound love she felt for an ex-boyfriend, someone who had taught her how to "fly"…and the traces of this love are preserved in "Antología."

In keeping with her Catholic beliefs, the singer has always held a clear antiabortion position. In the last song on *Pies descalzos*, "Se quiere…se mata," she narrates the turbulent story of a girl who dies as she is undergoing an abortion. In the song, due to the "law of magnetism," the girl has sexual relations with her boyfriend and gets pregnant. Without letting her parents or her boyfriend know, she decides to go for an abortion and ends up "dos metros bajo tierra viendo crecer gusanos" (six feet under, watching worms grow). It's the only dark and terrible story on the album, though the music is not as dark as the lyrics. According to the president of her fan club in Colombia, this song came to Shakira as a suggestion from her cousin, a devotee of the Virgin Mary who is said to receive messages from Mary on the thirteenth of every month. One of these messages, "No to abortion," was specifically directed at young people, and with the idea of spreading this message, the song "Se quiere …se mata" came to be.

But as with many balladeers, love is, inevitably, the never-ending source of inspiration and a recurring theme in her compositions. Luckily, perhaps because she is an avid reader, Shakira manages to avoid obvious metaphors and played-out words. She creates images and situations that bear the influence of some of her favorite poets: among them, Mario Benedetti, Oliverio Girondo, and Pablo Neruda.

Like the latter, she creates metaphors and utilizes elements of nature to make analogies; like Benedetti, she removes elements from their context and plays with everyday situations. "Déjame quererte tanto que te seques con mi llanto..." (Let me love you so much that you dry up with my tears); "Fría como una estatua de sal en un mausoleo de cristal" (Cold like a statue of salt in a mausoleum of crystal); "Te busqué por las calles, en dónde tu madre, en cuadros de Botero, en mi monedero, en dos mil religiones, te busqué hasta en mis canciones" (I searched for you in the streets, at your mother's house, in Botero's paintings, in my purse, in two thousand religions, I searched even in my songs).

THE PLANETS

"I'm a typical Aquarius."

When someone asks Shakira about her zodiac sign, something magazines frequently do, it is obvious from the artist's response that she's quite familiar with this age-old subject. "I believe that when a number of people are born during a specific era, cosmic factors and the position of the stars must have some sort of influence, the way the moon influences the oceans and plants,"she told a Colombian magazine. Even though she doesn't read her horoscope every day to find out what destiny has in store for her, she admits to having the personality of a typical Aquarius. As she herself allows, the characteristics of this sign have helped her enormously when it is time to create. In her words: "Aquarius women are very sensitive, we believe we can make things right in the world. It's a very humanitarian sign, and because of that I feel a great attraction to and a great passion for all things human. It's fair to say that if I had had the opportunity to go to college, I know I would have studied psychology, anthropology, archaeology, or any subject that deals with the mind and behavior of human beings. It is also a sign with a strong inclination toward the arts, with a very strong character."

This broad, inclusive, and tolerant vision Shakira has of the universe makes her self-applied label of "eclectic" very fitting. This artist seems to live on various levels, capable of having Catholic, zodiacal, and philosophical conceptions of the same phenomena. And she would be able to explain them in Spanish, Arabic, or English.

"ESTOY AQUÍ"

Shakira's voice was already known thanks to her song "Dónde estás corazón?" but when the single "Estoy aquí" started getting play on the radio, no one could turn it off. And not just in Colombia. Even though Sony wasn't planning on launching the album outside of Colombia, *Pies descalzos* crossed the borders and got to Venezuela, where it found an unexpected number of followers. The same thing occurred a couple of months later in Mexico, then in Ecuador, Chile…Wherever it went, it caught on, and the radio stations acceded to the listeners' wishes.

The same thing happened with the videos. "Dónde estás corazón?" and "Estoy aquí" began to play on MTV more and more until they climbed to the top positions. Thanks in part to the broad acceptance of this last video, *Billboard Magazine* gave Shakira her first cover with an article entitled "Cómo un video lanza a una artista" (How a video launches an artist).

On January 17, 1996, "Estoy aquí" was number one on the top 100 in Colombia for the thirteenth consecutive week and "Un poco de amor" was second. The Shakira phenomenon was just beginning.

What the artist surely didn't know then was that the video "Estoy aquí" had left a very good impression on the heads of her record company, more specifically on the division of Sony for Latin America, run by Frank Welzer. According to what Sony Colombia's head of marketing told *Semana,* Welzer had decided to promote Shakira throughout the southern hemisphere if *Pies descalzos* reached sales of 50,000—a figure which, according to the magazine, she reached in fifteen days. So, even if it weren't in the initial plans for the launch, it was very shortly crossing the borders into other Latin countries.

With the success that *Pies descalzos* was having in Latin America and in Mexico (a good test market), Sony decided to launch it in the United States, too, and introduce the Colombian to the Latino market here. That was how on February 2 Shakira got to the Radio and Music Convention in Los Angeles for the official launch of her record in the United States.

Although this first step into the North American market was promising, there was no indication that Shakira would resonate here the way she had in other countries. Either way, this coastal girl lives a day at a time, and at that moment, hearing her voice on the radio in her country several times a day was enough to make her happy. She had worked hard and was finally able to breathe comfortably. That summer, her powerful voice was taking over the airwaves of the entire continent, from the United States to Argentina.

"Ask and ye shall receive," goes one verse in the Bible, a text our artist knows well. The miracle that Shakira had asked of God upon the launch of her record had been granted…with interest. With only ten months on the airwaves, Shakira had sold…a million copies! In the United States, selling a million copies is relatively common, but in Colombia very few reach that number. In a country where American bands dominate rock music and pop, that the Barranquillera should sell a million copies was a bona fide miracle.

Shakira fever began in an unexpected way, taking everyone by surprise. After having forecast that sales would not exceed a quarter of a million, the executives from Sony were discovering that Shakira was going Gold and Platinum in several countries, including the United States.

When the total sales reached the famous seven-digit mark, Sony Music inaugurated a special award, the Diamond Prism, and named Shakira the Superstar of the Million Copies. In the official press release describing the event, the record company compared the Colombian phenomenon with the Canadian crooner Alanis Morissette, who the year before had taken the world by surprise and had sold millions of copies of her first work.

And the comparison was not so off the mark. By the end of the year Shakira had sold two million copies of *Pies descalzos*, and a couple of months later the total reached three million including the European, Asian, and Latin American markets.

The impressive figures were no more than a reflection of the level of popularity that Shakira had reached. Every time she appeared on a radio or television show, a high rating was assured. In September of '96, for example, when a popular television host, Darío Arizmendi, invited her to appear on his program *Cara a cara*, the show set a record in Colombia, reaching 36.6 points on the rating scale, an unprecedented number for that kind of program.

Those working with Shakira at that time could clearly see why she was enjoying so much success. She was stubborn with the record company when it came to defining her style, she was obsessive with her work while recording, and she was articulate at the moment of composition. And all that was combined with a strong sense of discipline and the joy that Shakira brings to her music.

She could pull on tight leather pants and be an aggressive rocker, or leave her hair long and straight to turn herself into a sweet balladeer. Beyond her image, she was finally beginning to live what she had dreamed of for so many years: she was a star on her own terms (even though she prefers to be considered "an artist, not a star").

PIES DESCALZOS EN ROUTE...

The show she put on in Bogotá in October of 1995 at the launching of *Pies descalzos* was the perfect warm-up for the tour that the record company planned for her when sales began to spike. As on the first night at the Teatro Nacional La Castellana, Shakira came out with her hair straight but messy, with leather pants and minimal makeup. From that night on she always had an acoustic guitar under her arm, a harmonica in hand, and her body completely given over to the rhythms of her songs.

The tour began in Ecuador. Venezuela, Peru, Puerto Rico, and the Dominican Republic were next...and she hasn't stopped since. Her bare feet touched every nation that invited her, and in each country she did more than one concert.

Each one of her shows was vibrant and solid, or at least that's what the critics said. Besides her voice, Shakira's stage presence was expanding in sensational ways. Though the stage has been her second home since she was ten, the artist launched *Pies descalzos* with a freshness and grace that she had never had in her prior shows. Instead of choreographed dances, she now improvised throughout the show, playing with her voice, screaming, and talking to the audience...always allowing herself to go where the music took her. Now she finally, undeniably, owned the stage. And the audience knew it and adored her for it. They sang along with her and danced, relishing her songs with her. And the number of fans began to multiply.

The Viña del Mar Festival of Songs

Viña del Mar was where Shakira received her first international award in 1992 when she was just a teenage contestant, full of dreams and with an uncertain future. Four years later, in February of 1996, she returned to the stage in northern Chile. However, this time she came as a special guest, to leave her fiery mark on the Chilean public.

This is how the columnist Álvaro García described Shakira's performance in Viña del Mar for the magazine *Cromos:*

"She seduces with reggae, with the sway of her hips, with her engaging facial expressions. She revisits her old passion for rock and roll. She tosses her black hair as if possessed by Janis Joplin. She stops. She caresses the words of her 'Antología', remembers someone she loved and, with a song, thanks that person for all the happy memories....

"She plays a small harmonica and suddenly she is a child again. She cries. Her tears are seen on the two huge screens on stage that reveal her every expression to all. The people of Viña del Mar, who four years before saw her as a timid participant, reaffirm their affection for the petite and sweet Barranquillera and deliriously sing along with her."

"The Biggest Concert in the History of Barranquilla"

That was how the newspapers announced the concert that Shakira had planned in the main stadium of her hometown. The excitement was extreme. It was going to be the first time that the Barranquillera performed in her native city, in the land that saw her grow up. And this family was dying to see its beloved daughter. Literally, unfortunately.

With and without tickets, more people than expected went to the concert that evening. Teenagers, especially young girls, were waiting in line for the doors of the stadium to open. But the moment they opened, things got out of control: a crowd of teens ran and pushed each other to try to grab the best spots. In the ensuing riot that lasted several minutes with the authorities unable to control it, two teens were trampled and they suffocated to death.

When the concert began, an uninformed Shakira started singing before the full house; they applauded her as though she were a goddess. More than 45,000 people danced and sang to each song, and the night had the joy of a great party.

During the show Shakira was completely unaware of what had happened. But when the concert was over, the news reached her at the hotel. She could not believe it. She was upset that no one had told her. She felt helpless and suffered a great deal of pain. She cried a lot. Only God knows what the artist felt that night. Given her extreme sensitivity and empathy, this was perhaps the saddest and darkest day of her career.

Those two teens were not the only victims of the hysteria. The day after the concert, a fifteen-year-old girl, upset because her mother had not allowed her to attend the concert, committed suicide. According to the main newspaper of Barranquilla, the girl went to the pharmacy, bought cyanide pills and a soft drink, and locked herself in her room. When her brother found her, she had taken a lethal dosage and lay dying on her bed. She was dead by the time she arrived at the hospital. She committed suicide because she had missed the chance to see the only meaningful thing in her short life: Shakira.

These tragic stories show the extent of the passion that Colombian teens have for Shakira. They chilled the singer to the bone and made her rethink the future. In the wake of these events Shakira seriously considered quitting. Even to this day, this remains a sensitive episode she rarely speaks about.

THE UNITED STATES OPENS ITS DOORS

This country fell at her feet from the beginning. When Shakira first stepped onto a stage in Miami, she did it before 5,000 people, with a show that lasted ninety minutes and left everyone wanting more. Some of her admirers, the vast majority women, had paid up to a hundred dollars to see her. Shakira did not disappoint. According to one critic, "she acted with the confidence of a veteran artist" and surprised everyone with her "dramatic movements (on a couple of occasions she got down on the floor with the microphone)" and with her mastery of the harmonica. "[She] conquered the newspaper reporters and the public with her sweetness, charm and spontaneity," said a Reuters correspondent in April of '97.

Only two weeks after the concert, *Pies descalzos* received its first award in North America. The Spanish edition of *Billboard Magazine* handed the Barranquillera three awards: Mejor Álbum del Año (Album of the Year) for *Pies descalzos*, Mejor Artista Nueva (Best New Artist), and Mejor Vídeo (Best Video) for "Buscando un poco de amor."

A week later, Univisión gave her two of its "Premios Lo Nuestro," prestigious awards in the Hispanic community: Artista Femenina del Año (Female Artist of the Year) and Artista Revelación del Año en el género pop y balada (Best New Pop Artist).

A month later, Shakira sold half a million copies of *Pies descalzos* in the United States and Puerto Rico and was the recipient of a gold record from the RIAA (the Recording Industry Association Awards). According to her record company, Shakira was the first Hispanic artist to reach that sales figure with her first record released in the United States. She also received five platinum records, which in the Latin market is granted for every 100,000 copies sold.

Brazil and the Remixes

September, the start of spring in the southern hemisphere, found Shakira flourishing in the least likely market: Brazil. Despite all predictions, the Barranquillera had sold 500,000 copies of *Pies descalzos* several months before landing in this vast country for her tour. Her songs and videos were so popular that Sony decided to launch a Portuguese compilation of her biggest hits. The result was *Shakira, The Remixes*, an album with songs remixed for dance clubs, including four of her hits sung in Portuguese, some disco, and some house music. Among the new versions of her songs were "Estoy aquí," "Dónde estás corazón?," "Un poco de amor," and "Pies descalzos, sueños blancos."

Shakira learned to sing in Portuguese and did it respectably, without losing any of the strength or subtleties of her voice. However, as she would later admit, her fans always seemed to prefer the original Spanish versions of the songs. As for sales, the record ended up selling more than 300,000 copies. As for *Pies descalzos* , it reached number 40 of the top 50 sellers. And according to *Semana,* "of the twelve million copies reserved for foreign artists [in Brazil], one million were for *Pies descalzos.*"

In addition to the Remix album, Shakira dedicated special attention to Brazil, the land of samba and bossa nova. Her tour through Brazil lasted over a month, during which time she visited fifteen cities, including Sao Paulo, Rio de Janeiro, and Bahia, and performed a total of twenty-three concerts to sold-out stadiums. According to the critics, the audience sang along from beginning to end, as if they knew perfect Spanish and had known Shakira for years.

During this exhausting month of September, Shakira discovered that she had an impressive number of fans and that language was not a barrier to their hearts. At the end of the month, one newspaper said that the Barranquillera had become an unprecedented phenomenon for a foreigner in Brazil and compared her success with Michael Jackson's popularity in his time.

THE PERFECT WRAP FOR *PIES DESCALZOS*

To cap a tour that had spanned months and taken her through cities she never imagined she would visit, Shakira returned to her roots. On tour, she traveled with her parents, showed up on time for every sound test, and rehearsed her entrances and exits with her musicians. She conducted herself like a professional, and both the public and critics fell in love with her. The successful tour had taken her far from Bogotá, but now, Shakira wanted to go home, where everything had begun. According to Víctor Manuel García, a journalist for the newspaper *El Tiempo*, on Saturday, October 11, 1997, the stadium El Campín de Bogotá was packed. There was an intense chill and a light rain, but that did not stop the Bogotanos from dancing and singing for two hours to Shakira's rhythms.

After circling the globe for twenty months with her songs, she finally landed in the city dressed in black, like a true rocker, to play for the more than 30,000 people who gathered worshipfully at her feet. "Idol…" the young men and women screamed to her as they raised their arms.

Shakira began the concert with "Vuelve." When it was time for "Un poco de amor" she took off her leather jacket and general hysteria ensued. "Y ahora estoy aquí, queriendo convertir los campos en ciudad…" (I am here to convert the countryside into a city), she sang, and euphoria burst forth. Shakira controlled the audience with the mastery of a veteran orchestra conductor. She knew what to say, how to manage the pacing of the show, and how to strut across the stage. "The time has come to walk barefoot," she said, and the audience stood as one.

"Songs are the memories of life. And I'm going to sing to you a little of mine." Thus she introduced "Antología." As Víctor Manuel García described, "Shakira levitated with success on her big night in Bogotá. She went back to her dressing room. Bathed in sweat, she locked herself in and gave herself to God for a couple of minutes."

While she was wrapping up her tour in Bogotá, on the other side of the planet her voice was beginning to be heard. *Pies descalzos* had launched in Japan and "Estoy aquí" was fighting for first place on the radio stations.

SHAKIRA AND LOVE

"I prefer a noble heart over a sterile intelligence."

Those who know her confirm that Shakira is romantic and a dreamer. Even her idea of love is idealistic, clearly much more spiritual than sensual. A Colombian journalist said of her: "She understands love as a pure exercise, as one of the most important of God's covenants, as an instrument of inspiration and creation." He went on to say, "As a matter of fact, there are people close to her who dare to speculate that she will only give herself in body and soul the day of her wedding." Only she knows whether this is true.

What is true is that Shakira maintains a strong and open communication with her parents, especially her mother. "They talk about everything, they talk about sex and about kisses, about intentions, and about men," said a close friend. Back then, every time she would date a guy, her parents made sure that they met him first.

Because of her image as "the girl next door," Shakira drew much attention when in early 1996 she started to go out with Puerto Rican actor, Oswaldo Ríos, a leading soap opera actor almost twenty years her senior. After a few short relationships, like the five months she spent with actor Gustavo Gordillo, a former member of the teen pop group Poligamia the artist seemed to be looking now for the maturity of a more experienced man. The gossip columnists say they met in Miami when they bumped into each other at a club, and after that they separated only to go to work. The truth is, they had met a year before in Colombia, at the party where Sony had presented her with the Diamond Prism after she had sold her first million copies. She impressed him, but that night he did not approach her.

They started going out just before Shakira turned twenty. She was in the middle of her *Pies descalzos* tour and was beginning the ascent of her career. Oswaldo was busy taping the soap opera *La viuda de blanco*. Even though he was a leading man, neither the press nor Shakira's fans liked him. They claimed he was using her fame to enhance his own.

But beyond the nasty rumors and the media's disapproval, the romance always seemed stable. As usual, whenever she went out with him she asked for her parents' permission, and they often went with her. Even under the chaperonage of Doña Nidia and Don William, Shakira and Oswaldo saw each other as much as they could. Sometimes she would visit him on the set of the soap; other times he came with her on her tour.

The love story ended in September of that same year, apparently when the singer returned to Brazil. The news made every celebrity magazine; it was received with cries of joy from all of her admirers and from the gossip columnists, who'd been following her every step with the robust Puerto Rican actor. Apparently, Shakira's parents and Oswaldo didn't get along especially well, and that would have been hard on the relationship. But the real reason for the break-up never came out.

After that, and for several months, Shakira's heart belonged only to her music, although, according to her own admission, her heart is constantly falling in love, and "there is always someone out there."

The truth is that during her relationship with Oswaldo the press was so invasive—with cameras, commentators, and comments—that it left Shakira with little desire to discuss the matter. Since then the singer prefers to talk about her relationships as passing situations, but without mentioning names whenever possible. At least until the story with Antonio de la Rúa unfolded.

PIES DESCALZOS, THE FOUNDATION

Shakira could not remember what it was that she had promised God in return for the sale of a million records, but at the end of the tour, she found an opportunity to pay back, in part, her debt to "the man upstairs." As soon as she returned to Bogotá and looked around, she realized that there were many people in dire need of help.

"Pies Descalzos is an association that was created at the end of 1997. We sponsor events with the purpose of raising funds that we divide among different foundations whose focus is to help the children of my country, whether for children with heart problems, with AIDS, with leukemia, children from the streets, or the children of soldiers who have died in combat." Thus Shakira introduced the Fundación Pies Descalzos.

With this foundation the artist found a way to assist the victims of the Armenian earthquake and of hurricanes George and Mitch, and to build hospitals and schools for low-income children. Unlike other artists who, after earning a lot of money, decide to establish a foundation as a kind of tax shelter, Shakira supported her foundation not just financially but with her physical presence, actually visiting the emergency locations and helping the victims at the critical times.

Even with a bright future awaiting her, Shakira demonstrated that her spirit was still intact. Fame and money had not changed her simple heart, her desire to listen to and serve people around her, or her search for God. In Shakira's words, "Fame is a question of temperature: it's cold when it elevates and separates, and it's warm when it brings people together and reminds you of your humanity. I have used it to get closer to my fans, not to get further away from them."

5

DÓNDE ESTÁN LOS LADRONES?

"I am a thief of attention, a thief of affection, a thief of realities."

To discover the Barranquillero soul, one has to understand the Carnivals of *La Arenosa*, the loving nickname given to Barranquilla. Noisy, colorful, and exuberant, these festivals have the entire town dancing and partying in the streets for three consecutive days. There are processions of people dressed in colorful costumes and cumbia groups along the Vía 40, raucous laughter and crowds until early morning hours, traditional costumes and perspiring people....It's the party of the year and no one wants to miss it. In the air are the notes of every tropical rhythm imaginable. Just as the samba is the blood of the Brazilian carnival and the street musicians are the soul of the carnival in the River Plate region, Barranquilleros express themselves with tropical rhythms: cumbia, salsa, merengue, vallenato....

Shakira was raised among all these rhythms. This is the music that surrounded her on the afternoons she spent playing outside. In neighborhoods of Barranquilla, music coexists in the street with the people. So it struck many as curious that the artist should favor rock and pop for her songs.

But Barranquilla is known to be a city of tolerance, embracing differences and diversity, and nowhere is this more apparent than in its music. This was evident at the Carnival of 1998, when Shakira was awarded the coveted El Super Congo de Oro. The Congo is usually reserved for those notable in the tropical genre, but that year an exception was made: the heads of the Carnival could not ignore the daughter of Barranquilla, the rocker who was Colombia's best ambassador. Shakira could not believe it. She got so emotional that February afternoon that when she sang with Joe Arroyo, at the height of the celebration, the classic song "Te olvidé," she cried with joy. Upon receiving the award she said, "This is like winning a Grammy." She did not know then that one day she would really be able to compare the experiences.

Here she was, just twenty-one years old, singing at the Carnival that had been her greatest delight as a child. Now, on the stage above the procession, she was the star influencing the style of a new generation. And all this despite the fact that she had spent the previous months working in Miami, and was hardly able to visit Barranquilla. Or, rather, not nearly as much as she wanted.

Like a bonus birthday gift, that same month she was decorated with the Orden al Mérito Nacional (National Merit Citation) from the President of Colombia, Dr. Ernesto Samper Pizano, who gave her the title of Goodwill Ambassador. Although this title was merely honorary, the Barranquillera has taken it very seriously. Whenever she travels, and since the success of *Pies descalzos* that's been often, Shakira feels that she is not only representing herself, she is also representing Colombia. "I believe that an artist is an example of her entire country, of the thoughts and feelings of a race and of a people. Therefore, as an artist, I have to try to make sure I am delivering the right message to the rest of the world," she said years later in a press conference, showing everyone how deep her sense of responsibility was.

A couple of months after being named "ambassador," Shakira took advantage of her European tour to visit Pope John Paul II, after having been granted a much coveted audience. She met him not only as a singer but also as a Colombian, so she could ask the head of the church for his intervention in the peace process in Colombia. As an offering she gave him a letter and a few typical gifts from her country, but she also asked for a favor. "I told him that it would be really nice if he would come by sometime," she confirmed, smiling a year later while confessing her request to Su Santidad.

As an ambassador and as an artist, in 1998 she traveled extensively: in early May she arrived in Monaco, where that year the World Music Awards were being held. At a formal dinner celebrities as varied as Mike Tyson, Roberto Carlos, and Mickey Rourke watched Shakira take the award for Bestselling Latin Artist. Appropriately enough, that night Gloria Estefan handed her the award.

That year couldn't have been more promising: after having received the blessing of his holiness John Paul II and the World Music Award, Shakira returned to Miami to continue the production of her next album, which was as yet untitled. Nor, in truth, did it have any songs. The only thing it had was a couple of finished songs, drafts of some lyrics, and maybe a few ideas for more songs, but not enough to take to the studio and start recording.

Shakira moved to Miami for the same reason that, years before, she had moved from Barranquilla to Bogotá. To grow. The difference was that this time she didn't have to pursue the press or pose in a bikini for a derriere contest. This time she was welcomed with open arms as the most important female artist for Sony Latin America...and with the best godfather a Latina artist could have in the United States—producer Emilio Estefan Jr.

Estefan was introduced to Shakira by her promoter and long time friend, Jairo Martínez. Jairo thought that Shakira's career could be boosted with the support of the number one producer in the His panic market, and after discussing it with Nidia, he decided to put them in touch to see what happened. According to Shakira, the chemistry was immediate, and after ten minutes of conversation she knew that she had found the producer of her dreams. For Estefan, the feeling was mutual. Shakira's undeniable magnetism compelled the producer to offer her the production services of Estefan Enterprises for her next album.

More meetings and conversations followed that first one. The truth is that Shakira needed several meetings in order to be able to intelligently and carefully negotiate the contract that she would sign with the most important producer in the Latin market. Shakira knew that her music needed not only the support of a great recording studio like Estefan's Crescent Moon, but her career also needed someone to open the doors to the U.S. market. And Estefan could offer all that. The question now was how to take such a big step, should she do it now or not, change managers or not, change her production crew or not. Will I have to give up some creative license and the decision-making power I've gained with the success of *Pies descalzos*, Shakira must have asked herself.

Until that moment the artist had found in Luis Fernando Ochoa an ideal producer, someone with whom she had great creative chemistry and with whom composing had been a pleasure. On the other hand, Emilio Estefan Jr. was an industry giant with twenty years of experience. In his roster of hits were records by stars like Gloria Estefan, Enrique Iglesias, and Thalía. If anyone knew how to produce Latin musicians and get them into the number one spot on the charts, it was Estefan. His contacts in Miami, the capital of Spanish-language music, were unsurpassed. And his opinion was highly regarded by Sony Music.

One of Shakira's concerns was having creative autonomy over her music. Emilio Estefan was renowned for being deeply involved, perhaps too involved, in the production of his records. So before signing their contract, the roles and duties were clearly defined. He would be her manager and her executive producer, but she would be in charge of all the material and arrangements and have approval over the final look of the records. Estefan would provide the logistical support, but the artist would retain creative control, and in addition could work with other producers for any particular song. She would be the captain of this ship, and that is indeed how it worked out, judging by her later comments.

The production of this record was considerably more complicated and demanding than that of *Pies descalzos*. There were more hands, more opinions, more producers, and more demos. The process took nine months, as long as a pregnancy. "To me it's a normal time, the gestation period for a baby," said Shakira, not denying that it was unusually long. "But many people wag their finger and tell me that the next one cannot take so long…," she concluded, chuckling.

But the record's delay was due not just to technical difficulties but to an unforeseeable and unfortunate interruption.

At the International Airport of Bogotá, while waiting for one of the many flights she was taking in late 1997, finishing up her *Pies descalzos* tour, Shakira's bag containing the songs for her next album was stolen. Stuffed in a binder in her bag was every single song written for her next record…and she didn't have copies. They were the scribbled originals with all of her marks right on the page. "The worst part about the whole thing was that I couldn't remember them because of the mental block that can be caused by such a traumatic experience as the robbery of such a personal item."

Feelings of impotence and emptiness overcame Shakira with such violence that for a couple of days and nights she thought of nothing but the thief or thieves who had taken her material. They had left her naked, incomplete, and confused. They had taken not only her songs, but also her thoughts, because now her mind could not stop thinking about the thieves, over and over again: Who are they? What were they looking for? Where are they?

Destiny had once again played a dirty trick, one that forced Shakira to have faith and confidence in herself and her destiny.

DÓNDE ESTÁN LOS LADRONES?

"For people who want to know who Shakira is, all they have to do is listen to Dónde están los ladrones? *There they will find my confessions."*

Shakira turned her most unfortunate experience into her biggest hit. She searched for a reason behind the theft of her songs, and her obsessed mind found an answer. "I came to the conclusion that there are all types of thieves," she later explained. "A thief is not just a person who takes a physical object that doesn't belong to him or her. There are thieves who steal feelings, space, time, dreams, rights." As if including herself in the indictment "let whoever is free of sin cast the first stone," Shakira concludes, "From that point of view, we all have stolen at one time or another, myself included. The dirty hands [on the cover of her album] represent the shared guilt. No one is completely clean, in the end we are all accomplices."

And stopping just short of calling her interviewer a thief, Shakira said, "I stole your questions, and you my answers." She even stated that music had stolen something from her. "It has stolen hours of sleep, unfinished breakfasts, sunsets I have not been able to see...."

Just before *Dónde están los ladrones?* was launched, *Pies descalzos* had sold over three and a half million copies worldwide, and "Estoy aquí" was still being played on radio stations throughout the continent. Making a new album in the wake of that success put a great burden on Shakira's shoulders. The critics, the press, and her fans naturally expected the new album to be better, more complex and forceful.

Also raising expectations was the cover that the Latin American edition of *Time* had dedicated to her. Next to her mischievous features and unbraided hair, the title of the cover read: "Era of the Rockera." With that Spanglish phrase, the article analyzed the phenomenon of Latin American women who were leaving their marks in the world of rock. Or in the United States, *rock en español*. *Time* called Shakira the "princesa del rock" and summarized her impressive career. Among the numerous achievements listed were the fact that the Colombian had sold almost four million copies of *Pies descalzos*, that she had written all her own songs, and that she played both the guitar and the harmonica marvelously.

Shakira knew that when it came to the reception of her next album, some would say that "she had changed too much" and others would reproach her if she remained the same. But at the moment of creation, her self-confidence triumphed. "All I could do was be myself. I understood that all I had to do was write the music I knew how to write and to write from the heart when I was compelled to. In that way, everything developed naturally, more so than I could have imagined," she said as she was putting the final touches on the record.

The artist put all of her energy into this record, polishing the material to the point of exhaustion. "I made two or three demos of each song. I became a human being so demanding of myself that until the song made my hair stand on end, I wouldn't stop." Each song was recorded with the same stubbornness and tenacity that she used to record the songs of *Pies descalzos*, because as she confessed in her song "Inevitable": "Conmigo nada es fácil, ya debes saber..." (With me nothing is ever simple, you should already know that).

And when the time came to enter the recording studio, her perfectionism fit Emilio Estefan's meticulous supervision like a glove. She later stated about her producer, "He had a great respect for me as an artist and trusted me totally on this project."

Nor did Shakira rest when it came to designing the videos, the cover of her album, and her own image. In keeping with her increasingly rocker sound, for this album she left her hair loose and messy and filled it up with little colorful braids. She looked like a modern Medusa who could bewitch her audience with furious movements of her head and the frenetic body movements of a possessed soul. But unlike the mythological Medusa that would turn into stone anyone who dared to stare at her, this one couldn't petrify anyone. On the contrary, her power consisted of making the whole world, even the most inflexible stone, throb and dance. She had turned into an aggressive and untamed rocker. And everyone, both fans and critics, loved her new image, because in essence she was still sensitive and sweet.

As Shakira once said when asked how she would define her music, "My music is fusion, a combination of elements that come from different worlds but that live harmoniously under the same roof." That fusion, which according to Shakira is gold for Latinos, a shared treasure, was the key element in the construction of *Dónde están los ladrones?* "For example, in 'Ciega sordomuda' I combined the typical Mexican trumpets with a disco dance loop and an electric guitar. In 'Octavo día' there is more of a British influence, and in 'Ojos así' there are Middle Eastern instruments, and, again, a dance loop and the electric guitar."

Just as Shakira has no problem recognizing the extent to which she has been influenced by different musical styles and that she is a living example of fusion herself, she is also eclectic when it comes to choosing the subjects of her songs. The artist opens up spiritually and allows her views on God to speak for themselves in the song "Octavo día," offers political criticism in "Dónde están los ladrones?", and confesses an infidelity in "Inevitable." The texture of her videos also changes with each song, and in each one you can see the desire to innovate both aesthetically and dramatically.

On September 7, 1998, after she had spent almost three years writing thousands of lines on small scraps of paper and being locked up day and night in the recording studio for a few months, Shakira's voice burst onto the radio with the first single off the new record: "Ciega sordomuda." Almost instantly, Hispanic radio stations in the United States were playing it endlessly. With this single appetizer, the critics were already saying, "The sound of the production is excellent and it's got all the right things to become the bestselling rock-pop album in the world," and they were not wrong.

When *Dónde están los ladrones?* was launched on the twenty-third of that same month, hundreds of critics were invited to attend the press conference and launch party in Miami. Unlike the low budget Shakira had for *Pies descalzos*, several hundred thousand dollars was spent on the promotion; the record company even paid for the air travel of foreign journalists.

Proving that she was worthy of the noble title that *Time* had given her, Shakira sold more than 300,000 copies of *Dónde están los ladrones?* the day it was launched. The pressure of fans who wanted to hear the latest from their rocker "princess" was so great that several stores opened their doors at midnight to satisfy the demand. By the end of the month over a million copies had been sold and Shakira became the bestselling Latina artist.

With a more fully developed vocal range and a more defined personality, Shakira presented the fourth album of her career and bared her soul in every song. And you didn't have to be an intimate friend to realize that several of her lyrics were autobiographical. Like the previous album, a recurring theme is love in all of its manifestations. But unlike *Pies deszcalzos,* the woman on this album is stronger, more determined, and more aggressive. For example, she lets us know that "Si me cambias por esa bruja, pedazo de cuero, no vuelvas nunca más, que no estaré aquí" (If you leave me for that dirty, cheap witch, don't even bother coming back, 'cause I won't be here), in "Si te vas."

Musically the spirit is more rebellious, harsher, than in the previous record. To the mixture of the pop, rock, and disco sounds she added one truly original song, "Ojos así," which is sung half in Spanish and half in Arabic and combines desert images and Middle Eastern rhythms, which helped to distinguish the album from any other.

Emilio Estefan was more than satisfied. He could not find enough words to praise Shakira or describe how magnificent it was to work with "someone who knows what she wants, who is a perfectionist, and above all a hard worker." He added, "She reminds me of Gloria, they are two very, very intelligent women." He was so sure that Shakira would become the next Latin sensation, the new Ricky Martin, that almost as soon as *Dónde están los ladrones?* came out, he told the press that an English version of the same album was in the works. He even had his wife, Gloria, help Shakira translate some of the lyrics.

Shakira expressed more than once how supported she felt working with him. Emilio had given her the absolute creative freedom that she needed, making sure, as well, that the resources and people she required were at her disposal. And that support made the record the meticulously crafted final product that Shakira had envisioned.

This was a very important record for her career for various reasons. First of all, with it she proved to her fans that she wasn't a fleeting star and that her prior success was not mere coincidence. In this new production, she kept the romantic ballads, but with a more confident and harsher edge, with a more produced sound and a fusion of original rhythms. Besides, the variety in her vocals left no doubt: Shakira was evolving at breakneck speed.

The second reason was the people who had yet to discover her. Although she was a heavyweight in Latin America and many European countries and the Middle East, the United States remained just out of reach. But now, with a an album recorded and mixed entirely in Miami, with Emilio Estefan Jr. as executive producer and the formidable financial support of Sony, Shakira had a real opportunity to make it in the United States. This market was keeping an eye on her and predicted a promising future, much like that of Ricky Martin.

"THE STYLE HAS CHANGED BUT THE CONTENT IS STILL THE SAME"

With her messy hair, almond eyes, and "dirty hands," Shakira insisted that her metamorphosis was not just skin deep, but that her essence remained the same. "I'm open to metamorphosis," she said. The makeover logically followed the change in her music: her eyes had the look of an Arabic woman, appropriate for singing "Ojos así," and her long, colorful hair gave her a contemporary hippie look for songs like "Ciega sordomuda."

With the launch of *Dónde están los ladrones?*, she endured exhausting workdays with the press. For several days Shakira did nothing but grant interviews, do photo shoots, and talk in front of all sorts of cameras. With the serenity of a Buddha, the artist listened to every question and answered each one attentively. She would think for a moment and then respond, trying to make the conversations agreeable and fresh, even if she had to answer the same questions thirty times: "Where was the suitcase full of her songs taken, what kind of things inspire her, her Lebanese ancestry…" Shakira searched deep inside herself to find original, or at least somewhat profound, responses.

In discussing her lyrics, she explained, "For me, singing about the manifestations of love is inevitable. That marvelous feeling that seduces us into a hypnotic trance, like in 'Ciega sordomuda,' or forces us to give up everything, like in 'Tú,' makes us believe solely in the person we love, as in 'No creo,' makes it difficult for us to forget, as in 'Sombra de ti'…But my songs include social views as well. That is the case in 'Octavo día' and 'Dónde están los ladrones?' which, with a dose of humor or irony, question certain attitudes that we frequently see."

Returning to her origins and living up to the meaning of her name, "woman of grace," Shakira ended the record with a song, sung in Arabic and Spanish, that seems to have been born in the deserts of the "Arabian Nights." "Ojos así" is a tribute to her Lebanese ancestors and in short order became her personal signature. "One of my most precious dreams is to perform one day in Lebanon," she said in one of her many interviews.

As for the soul of the record, what she said is true: the heart of her music had not changed. She continued to sing about love with ballads and the rhythms of "rock and pop, or pop and rock, I wouldn't know which to put first." However, that record was her first major step in the American market, so any comparison to previous albums was not much of a concern. This would be her calling card.

While she was promoting her record, journalists continuously asked her about the origin and inspiration of her songs. She'd say that poetry enriched her spiritually and intellectually. For example, she was reading Mario Benedetti, Jaime Sabines, Pablo Neruda...but when the time came to write her songs she had no idea how they came to light. The inspiration continued to seem like a miracle. For example, she said, with "Octavo día" at first she had only two paragraphs and the music, nothing more. But while taking a shower very late one night and not even thinking about the song, she got the first paragraph of the second verse and then the second paragraph, and had to come running out of the shower. "I think I receive faxes," she said, suggesting that it was God himself faxing her all the material.

6

THE FIRST STEPS TO A CROSSOVER

"Although it might help me, I don't feel like part of that explosion. I've always done rock and pop; my sound is not Latin...."

Though Shakira already had a reputation for being obsessive about everything regarding her music, nothing demonstrated just how meticulous she could be until she started studying English. She had spent the last months of '98 studying the language, trying to smooth out her choppy pronunciation and accent, reading books and watching movies. She practiced so much during the day that at times she dreamed in English. She was demanding an extraordinary amount from herself. She had admitted more than once that her native language was Spanish and that she couldn't compose in any other language. "My poetic resources are extracted from Spanish, which is a Latin language and is more romantic. English is more rigid, more practical and direct, and the ideas are more direct in that language. And I'm neither simple nor practical," she said. That is why the task of translating some of her songs was left to Gloria Estefan.

Shakira always thrived on challenges, but recording in English was a major challenge. She had already sung in Portuguese for *The Remixes* album, and she did it well, with good pronunciation and diction. But this new language was much harder to master, even though she had studied it back in Catholic school.

Despite her dedicated preparation, when it was time for Shakira to make her English debut, she became panic stricken. In early 1999, Rosie O'Donnell invited her to appear on her popular daytime talk show, to sing for the first time in English for a television audience. That day, instead of O'Donnell, Gloria Estefan would introduce her. Like a mother taking her daughter to school on the first day, Gloria would present the rocker to her new audience. The pressure and the demands told her that she wasn't ready. She hardly slept before the show, she shed more than one tear, and she suffered a fever—all because of her nervousness. When she got to the studio she felt sick and had a sore throat. "It was one of the most exhausting times in my life," she told Gabriel García Márquez in an interview for his magazine *Cambio*. "I cried almost the entire night because I didn't think I could do it."

Nevertheless, on January 28, 1999, a little after 10:00 a.m., Shakira started to sing the first verses of her song "Inolvidable," and all the fears, doubts, and dilemmas disappeared. In their place was left her clear and energetic voice, singing in clean and perfect English. Her voice was just as strong in English as it was in Spanish, and Gloria Estefan heaped lavish praise on her. That morning, her debut on ABC left everyone satisfied.

Shakira's performance was perhaps the first ripple of the looming Latin wave. On February 24, during a relatively boring Grammy Awards, a Puerto Rican fired up the television screens in the United States with his song "La copa de la vida." Rosie O'Donnell, who, coincidentally, was hosting the show that night, was impressed. "I never heard of him before tonight, but I'm enjoying him so-o-o much," she said when Ricky Martin finished his number. The following day, the records of the Puerto Rican sensation flew out of stores, even in places like Salt Lake City, famous for its vast Mormon community more inclined toward religious music than pop. Stores had to reorder more Ricky Martin records for their racks.

Ricky Martin's success that night belonged not just to him, but to the entire Latin pop community. As O'Donnell had indicated, there were a lot of people who had no idea who he was. Millions of viewers were seeing him for the first time in their lives, yet they couldn't help but jump to their feet and start dancing. Beyond Ricky Martin's sensuality and his professional performance was something more: the music, the beat, the frenzy of Latin pop. And he was the first to cross over to mainstream America, practically overnight.

This talented Puerto Rican started to rise on the charts, making way for what would be called the Latin Boom, a boom that turned out to be more than just a passing fad. Thanks to the success of this performance, Sony Discos, with Tommy Mottola at the helm, decided to break out the drums and cymbals to introduce its Latin pop stars to the American market. The company bet heavily on the talents who were already recognized in Latin markets and invested millions of dollars to hire new producers with knowledge in the crossover field. That's why rapper and producer Sean "Puffy" Combs, the creator of Notorious B.I.G., was called in to produce songs for Jennifer Lopez, and Canadian David Foster, former keyboard player for John Lennon and composer-producer of many hits, was brought in to produce Luis Miguel. So too with the masterly touch of great producers, were the first English records of Marc Anthony and Jennifer Lopez launched. Anthony already had a solid career in the New York salsa scene, and she was an established actress but was new to the music scene.

Among this small group that Sony was heavily backing, Shakira had the highest Latin American sales. The Colombian had proved that she could be number one in Latin America, including Brazil, and in Europe, Asia, and the Middle East. As if sales weren't enough, in various countries such as Spain, Turkey, and Argentina, girls were copying Shakira's style. In almost every school, girls were colorfully braiding their hair and wore friendship bracelets, and they were wearing out the album. They adored that end-of-the-century hippie look, and they identified with the love stories she constructed with uncomplicated poetry. Why wouldn't she also prevail in the American pop scene?

Coincidentally or not, the territory had been meticulously prepared, and when the time came to make the jump, Shakira was ready. *Dónde están los ladrones?* put Shakira on the covers of *Cosmopolitan, Seventeen, Glamour* and *Latina*, took her to number one on the Billboard charts, and had the *Miami Herald* talking. All of this and she had not even gone on tour. This record also gave her her first Grammy nomination. Even the critics praised the record. "The buzz around Shakira is justified," said Christopher John Farley in his *Time* magazine review of *Dónde están los ladrones?* "Missing out on this collection should be deemed a misdemeanor, at least."

As a songwriter, Shakira won her first Latino Billboard awards for the songs "Ciega sordomuda," "Tú," and "Inevitable." That year, for the first time in the history of the award, there were five winning composers, each with three songs to his or her credit. That was the year "Livin' la vida loca" left with all the major awards, including Song of the Year, for being the song most listened to according to the Billboard charts.

"Ciega sordomuda" stayed on the Hot Latin Tracks for several weeks while Shakira attended photo sessions for women's magazines or went to recording studios to be interviewed. In the articles written about her, all the interviewers seemed surprised by her humility, her maturity, and her reverence toward God and respect for her parents.

They were also surprised to see that Shakira had not only a fabulous voice but an admirable mind as well. Some discovered for the first time that she wrote her own songs, and time and time again they used the comparison that *USA Today* had coined when it introduced her as the "Latina Alanis Morissette." The comparison caught on. After all, the U.S. market is not used to having this type of foreign singer who, armed with a guitar, is able to set the entire stage on fire with the power of her voice. So, when discussing Shakira, it was almost impossible not to compare her to the Canadian artist, who had a similar image: a small physique, long black hair, and a guitar always in hand.

But Shakira would not allow herself to be compared. With brutal honesty, she expressed pride in her Arab roots and her Catholic religion, admitted to being "a walking contradiction," and confessed to a total dependence on God. What other rock artist could say such a thing? She set herself apart in the rock world and justified it by saying that "rock is an attitude, it's the way I express my frustrations and my sense of impotence." With those words Shakira broke with the cliché that rockers have to be aggressive and violent to be taken seriously.

So she won over the critics and charmed the women's and music magazines. Dressed in Arab attire or in leather pants, either with colorful braids or her hair down and messy, her image was everywhere. The magazine *People en español* voted her among the most beautiful women of 1999, and *Seventeen* said, "even if you don't understand a word of Spanish, you will love her musical mixtures and the adrenaline rush this artist produces." And along with the encouraging reviews, the sales of her record multiplied and the first awards began to roll in. In April of 1999 she received the Billboard Latin Music Award for Best Pop Album and in May she received two Premios Lo Nuestro, one for Artista Femenina (Female Artist) and one for Álbum del Año (Album of the Year).

In the meantime, her own country had not forgotten her. In May of that year, the magazine *TV y Novelas*, the one that many say helped her get started, declared her the Colombian Artist of the Century. Shakira flew to Bogotá and arrived at the awards show an hour and a half late, to an ecstatic audience. When she went on stage to accept the award, she showed her facility for winning over an audience. "Right here I have something that makes me feel even prouder than my songs do, something I'm prouder of than all my awards and all the admiration from the public," she said waving a small black handkerchief with something inside. There was suspense in the room. When she opened the handkerchief, she took out something that looked like a little notebook: it was her Colombian Passport. "I'm proud to be Colombian," she declared. The applause was deafening.

Shakira was crossing over very gradually, and she appeared to have some worries about losing her Colombian fans. Did she fear that singing in English or living in the United States would make her less Colombian? That may be why she took a while to acknowledge that she was living in Miami and not in Bogotá: for several months she lived in both places, but slowly she started to settle in Florida. Though she lives there almost year round when she is not traveling, she has never given up her house in Bogotá or her occasional visits to Barranquilla. Even if these visits are becoming less frequent, Shakira always remembers that her heart is in Colombia, "a land that never forgets how to smile."

She always knew achieving her dreams would entail a lot of sweat and tears, especially for someone as sensitive as she is (according to an old friend she, "cries over everything"). Now, her career was forcing her to establish her residence in Miami, to not have time to swim or ride horseback (two things she loves to do), and to spend many hours on airplanes. But to put things in perspective, she was now playing in the big leagues.

SHAKIRA, THE IMAGE OF THE NEW GENERATION.

Dónde están los ladrones? had sold more than three million copies worldwide when Pepsi offered Shakira her first multimillion-dollar contract. Aware of the Latin Boom, by the middle of 1999 the executives of the "taste of a new generation" wanted Shakira and Ricky Martin to be the faces for their next publicity campaigns in Latin America and the United States. The brand that years before had sponsored giants like Michael Jackson, Madonna, and Tina Turner and which, more recently, sponsored the Britney Spears tour, was betting heavily on Shakira's career.

But Pepsi was not the only business to notice the power that Shakira's music had with young people. MTV was already playing her videos throughout Latin America and knew how popular she was there. Catching the wave of popularity that her latest album had created, the cable station asked her to do an acoustic concert, one of its famous *MTV Unplugged* shows. This placed Shakira among the privileged fourteen Latin American artists—along with the groups Maná and Café Tacuba—to have done this kind of concert.

A performance like this was a great challenge for Shakira, who was very proud of her electronically produced dance beats. But these are the kinds of challenges she loves. "The challenge was not to let the energy of the songs drop, but simply to make an acoustic version of them and to modify the arrangements just slightly." What she did was work with some of the musicians who had accompanied her on her latest album, in order to modify the arrangements of some of the songs and add new sounds to others.

Some of those who returned to work with her were Tim Mitchell, as artistic producer, Luis Fernando Ochoa, and the drummer Brendan Buckley. As always, Shakira was involved in everything, from the selection of songs to the new arrangements and instruments, and more.

In designing the set, Shakira also had some ideas: Why not fill up the stage with wild animals, such as tigers and snakes, while she sang? The producers of the concert implored her to find an alternative, since a concert like that would be too dangerous. Without making much of a fuss, Shakira looked for other, less controversial designs, and completely dedicated herself to reworking her songs, which would fill up the stage better than any wild animal.

When everything was ready, on the afternoon of August 12, 1999, MTV opened the doors of the Manhattan Center Grand Ballroom in New York. A select group of people came in, the majority of them fans, to watch this atypical show. Shakira was impeccably dressed in black, with leather pants and a simple shirt, red sparkles in her hair, and a little nervous tremble in her body. All it took were the first chords of "Octavo día," and her nerves disappeared. There she was, stripped of everything and radiating light. As always, her charisma and presence made this concert a magical event. The spectators were uncontrollable; they screamed to their idol and celebrated each one of her words. Some of those words were gentle confessions, as in "Sombra de ti," which was born "at four o'clock in the morning, in the recording studio with all the lights turned off and my heart broken."

The only things missing on the set were the wild animals. As for everything else, the acoustic show had everything anyone could want: intimacy, energy, and serious chemistry. The show opened with "Octavo día" and was followed by the wild "Dónde están los ladrones?" and the heartwarming "Inevitable," which revved up the audience. As a special guest the mariachi group "Los Mora Arriaga" came to "add a little taste of guacamole" to "Ciega sordomuda." A new instrument, the dumbek, a small Arab drum, marked the beat of "Ojos así," the song that electrified the night.

The guests screamed, sang, and danced along with her. Everyone, absolutely everyone, was satisfied with the concert—the audience and the producers. At the end of the night, Shakira gave an emotional farewell: "You have given me a marvelous night." For the staff of MTV, this was one of the quickest and easiest concerts they had produced.

The positive reaction to the *Unplugged* concert in Latin America and the United States made MTV and Sony decide to turn it into a record for international distribution. While the studio versions of "Ciega sordomuda," "Tú," and "Inevitable" were still being played on the radio, the acoustic versions on *MTV Unplugged* were launched, giving Shakira a new voice in the market.

By the end of the year Shakira knew that she needed to perform live. She missed the contact with her audience and promised them that she would soon go back out on tour. It was taking longer to make those live concerts happen, not because of Shakira, nor her manager, nor Sony Discos, but because of her popularity. Her schedule was jam-packed with obligations that she had to fulfill. She was experiencing the consequences of crossover success. She was going from one interview to another and from one airplane to the next.

Before the year ended, for example, Shakira returned to Colombia, but not for a concert. In November she arrived in Cartagena to sing at the Miss Colombia contest. She had changed her hair again, this time to blonde, and had kept a few braids. She sang three songs, including "Ciega sordomuda," and she closed the show with a brilliant interpretation of "Ojos así." According to one reporter, Shakira received more applause than the contestants.

When she spoke to the public she emphasized where her heart was: "I always, always think about all of you; I always, always think about my country, because I love you all." Returning to Colombia made her nostalgic. She needed to assure her people that the love she had for them was intact, that she would always "belong to them," regardless of her work obligations or place of residence.

Also near the end of the year, MTV Latin America viewers voted Shakira their second favorite female artist, after Madonna. This second place gave her the chance to host the program "Mujeres Arriba" in which MTV presented the best female rock and pop artists, women who were leaving their mark in history. Several years younger and with a career still on the rise, Shakira was situated comfortably close to the indisputable queen of pop, the chameleonic Ms. Ciccone.

Her second multimillion-dollar sponsorship contract came from another youth-oriented company. Calvin Klein asked her to model for its successful ad campaign that presented musicians dressed in their jeans. The models were all up-and-coming, critically acclaimed musicians. In the United States the campaign began with Liz Phair, but then they decided to go with less-known stars such as Joshua Todd of Buck Cherry, Lisa Lopes of TLC, and Macy Gray (then almost unknown to the mainstream). As the only Latin American in the group, Shakira put on the jeans and was photographed by Steven Klein, allowing her to position herself among North American stars on the rise.

With her overbooked press and publicity calendar, the recording of her English album, the highly publicized crossover, was behind schedule. At first it was announced for the middle of '99, but now *MTV Unplugged* would come out before it and there was no date set for the recording of the new album.

During the delay of the English album, Shakira decided to change managers. Some journalists speculated that there was an argument between the artist and Emilio Estefan Jr., that the relationship had become rancorous because of a conflict of interest. While there may or may not be any truth to these rumors, what is certain is that Shakira broke with Estefan and signed with one of the most coveted managers in the business—Freddie DeMann. Explaining the change, Shakira said that her career "needed someone who could dedicate twenty-four hours a day to me, and Emilio does have other projects."

Freddie DeMann had been Michael Jackson's and Madonna's manager; he managed the latter for fourteen years. He knows the market as very few do and has a sixth sense when it comes to recognizing stars. In the choice of her new representative, Shakira once again proved that she was playing in the big leagues. After working with Emilio Estefan Jr. for almost two years, she now had a man with all the necessary contacts and power to take her to the international market. With Shakira's projected sales and the extension of her image, everything seemed to indicate that she was outgrowing Miami and the rest of the Latin markets.

But during this change in management, Shakira was taking her time composing her next album, which she had announced would be half-English, half-Spanish. Also before the year ended Shakira began to plan her promised tour around Latin America and Europe.

Now she was beginning to savor true success: She had been named Artist of the Century in Colombia, nominated for a Grammy, and had dozens of her records go gold and platinum, plus one multi-platinum record in the United States. On the brink of a crossover, she had a taste of how exhausting her career could be. As always, the days left time for nothing but work. "Time is mean and merciless," she stated, and as for romantic liaisons, that year there were very few, if any...or at least none that Shakira wanted to talk about.

7

WHERE IS SHAKIRA?

"I just want to make an album that will be as honest in English as it is in Spanish."

Shakira spent the New Year of 2000 in Barranquilla, surrounded by family and close friends. The new millennium found her wearing Calvin Klein jeans and drinking Pepsi. The only place where she appeared relaxed and still was on the giant billboards that decorated the principal cities across the world. In reality, the pop star was running around more than ever. She continued to be completely dedicated to her work, and her overbooked schedule left few days of rest. Right after celebrating the New Year she had to fly to Buenos Aires to film a commercial for the mobile phone company Nokia, the Japanese enterprise that was sponsoring her tour. She took advantage of her time there to do one concert and some interviews with the press. A couple of days later, she would begin her much anticipated tour, which would take her to fourteen different cities during the course of a month and a half. In the middle of her tour she had to fly to Spain and Paris for some small concerts, and begin promoting the *MTV Unplugged* album, which would be launched in February.

Indeed, this new year was promising to be an exhausting one, though not just with respect to work: Shakira began the year with an identity crisis. "I'm going through a really insecure period. Even if many don't believe it," she admitted in Buenos Aires. Perhaps as a way to reaffirm her personality, she radically changed her appearance. "Here you go," she told the journalist while touching her hair, recently dyed platinum and golden blonde. "A lot of people told me, 'No, Shakira is brunette.' Jeez! I am not my hair, I believe that I've overcome that fear." But the reporter had not even mentioned her hair. At that moment, her old image, the one with the black and red hair, was being imitated in cities all over the world, which should have diminished her insecurities.

However, her fans weren't paying attention to her fears. During the filming for the Nokia commercial in Buenos Aires, word that Shakira was in town, though incognito, spread like wildfire. A short time later, so many fans gathered around the site for the day's shoot that she was unable to leave her trailer and the filming had to be delayed. Even though this sort of incident was nothing new to her, she realized now that she was no longer interested in attracting attention, and that everywhere she went she preferred to whisper so that no one would recognize her.

It was during this insecure phase that she saw a James Bond movie and came to a realization: "Millions and millions of dollars are spent on a movie to distract us for an hour and a half. Absurd, isn't it? But that's what we live for, for distractions. And I worry; is that what's going on in my concerts as well?," she asked the reporter from *Gente* magazine. "I'm trying to do more than that." Then, as if consoling herself, "Art is something more than entertainment."

Considering that Shakira was about to enter the American market with her first English album, it was only understandable that she would experience some insecurity. The concept of crossing over, creating a product in a different language to widen your audience, creates a dilemma for any smart singer-songwriter: is she singing in English to grow professionally, or is she betraying her artistic credibility by pandering to the needs of the market? For an artist who prides herself on the honesty of her songs and who says she sings only what she feels, it is only logical that the thought of composing in English and for a new audience would provoke at least some anxiety.

That she had been constantly traveling for a year and a half may not have helped matters. She had become a nomad, as she would say. She lived in Colombia, Miami, aboard airplanes, in hotels....She had a hard time figuring out where home really was. But in February she returned to Miami to launch the *MTV Unplugged* album, her first live record, the only one so far that captured the excitement of her concerts. "This acoustic concert will give Shakira the opportunity to present herself as a complete artist," said Emilio Estefan Jr. during the presentation of the record, dispelling the rumors of quarrels between Shakira and her manager. "She will definitely leave a mark with her artistic ability."

The album was launched before a huge press conference. With her hair straight, taking just the right amount of time, Shakira gave a press conference in which she answered every conceivable question. Among other things, the reporters wanted to know the reason behind her change of management. There she confirmed that what she needed was someone who could dedicate himself to her full-time. "I would love to have Emilio in my future productions. [He and Gloria] are like my second parents." And with that she buried the idea that there was ever a vicious dispute between her and her ex-manager (who likewise denied what some columnists wrote but never confirmed, a story of creative egos in conflict). What was true was that Gloria Estefan had translated a few of Shakira's songs and that Estefan Enterprises would once again assist Shakira on her next album, which this time would be recorded, in part, in a studio in Nassau, the capital of the Bahamas.

ANFIBIO TOUR

The Anfibio tour, announced by Shakira a couple of months earlier, would begin in Panama City in March and from there would hit the major cities of eleven different Latin American countries, to finish off in Miami and San Diego. Many days before her concert in Uruguay, the tickets were gone. In these countries Shakira is not considered part of the Latin boom; as the leading newspaper in Uruguay, *El País*, wrote, "Shakira has an explosive mix that combines commercial ability with talent and artistic honesty."

Starting on March 17, Shakira performed in packed stadiums and theaters of different sizes. The audience invariably sang along to all fifteen songs in her repertoire, screamed out that she was their idol, and applauded until they were exhausted. On stage the presence of the now blonde star was extraordinary. Dressed in tight leather pants and a cropped blouse, her body would be taken over by the music, and she completely dominated the stage. Her band, which had some of the same musicians who had accompanied her on the *Unplugged* album, added a rock edge to the songs…and to her movements. Shakira, with her voice and her grace, took care of the rest.

The artist carefully chose the term *anfibio* (amphibious). After shuffling through several names, she selected this one as the one that truly defined her: a dual woman, very earthy but also viscerally connected to the water element, capable of adapting and willing to "metamorphose." Exemplifying these qualities, Shakira did not stay in the pop mold: in addition to the repertoire that everyone already knew, she included one song that she had always adored. She sang, practically a capella, "Alfonsina y el mar," an Argentinean song inspired by the romantic and tragic life of the poet Alfonsina Storni and made famous by Argentine folk singer Mercedes Sosa. "I heard this song when I was a little girl at a competition in my school. I was so overwhelmed, so surprised…it touched something deep inside me. And then when I learned the story behind the song, all the more." In other words, the concerts on the Anfibio Tour went through many different moods filled with rock rhythms, acoustic ballads, and dance music.

The concerts began with the first chords of "Dónde están los ladrones?," at which time she came out, moving and twisting inside an ovoid membrane. "I am a girl from a Third World country….And I'm proud of that," and the song continued. With her powerful voice enhanced by her guitar and harmonica, she was able to change the texture of her songs the same way she had done for MTV: she sang an acoustic version of "Mosca en la casa", "Ciega sordomuda" had the spirit of a ranchera, and "Ojos así" left a taste of deserts and camels on stage. Devouring the words to "Estoy aquí," Shakira would make her first, false exit. The applause and shouts brought her back on stage for her encore "Sombra de ti," a song that ended up being her favorite, and "No creo."

Between mid-March and the end of April 2000, this was Shakira's agenda, not including her last concerts in Buenos Aires which wrapped up the tour:

March 17:	Panama City, Panama
March 19:	Quito, Ecuador
March 21:	Lima, Peru
March 23:	Montevideo, Uruguay
March 25, 26, 27, and 28:	Buenos Aires, Argentina
March 30:	Santiago, Chile
April 2:	Caracas, Venezuela

April 4:	Valencia, Venezuela
April 5:	Maracaibo, Venezuela
April 7:	Bogotá, Colombia
April 9:	San Juan, Puerto Rico
April 12 and 13:	Mexico City, Mexico
April 16:	Guatemala City, Guatemala
April 19:	San Diego, California
April 20:	Anaheim, California
April 22:	Miami, Florida

There was some criticism of the tour, primarily the overselling of tickets in Guatemala, which according to the press could have caused a real tragedy; the long delays at the start of the show; the short duration of the show; and the accusation of the use of prerecorded music in Puerto Rico. The press complained that some of the ticket prices were too high, and because of that many fans were unable to see her. But according to the organizers this last complaint was due to the "Shakira phenomenon," which had grown faster than anticipated.

Because of all the people who couldn't get tickets, Shakira extended her tour, which was supposed to have ended in Miami. Instead, due to the insistence of the organizers in Buenos Aires, Shakira ended her tour there, in the Campo de Polo in front of 40,000 people.

This tour didn't just get all of Latin America talking about Shakira; it also earned her a position in the list of Top 50 Tours that the magazine *Pollstar* published in the summer of 2000. According to this magazine, which specializes in concerts and tracks the performances of various artists in the United States and the rest of the world, in July of 2000 there were only four Latinos whose tours ranked among the top fifty in attendance: Ricky Martin, Luis Miguel, Marc Anthony, and Shakira.

For the Anfibio Tour Shakira had a staff of thirty-two people and was constantly accompanied by her parents or her brother Tonino. William and Nidia waited for her at the end of every concert and helped her with whatever she needed before returning to the hotel together. As always, she prayed before getting on any stage and thanked God and her fans for the night they'd shared. A reporter who interviewed Shakira and her parents after one concert participated in the celebration in Shakira's dressing room. Nidia Ripoll, always traditional, wanted to point out to the reporter that "although it may sound boring, the girl has not changed." Since they were in Argentina, William Mebarak could not help but start singing tango and imitating local personalities. All the while Shakira laughed hysterically: "Papa, you never stop." A while later Shakira ended her interview reciting a poem by Oliverio Girondo.

AMOR WITH A CAPITAL A, FROM ARGENTINA

"I think I've been in love and I think I've loved, but not with a capital L, not yet." —*Shakira, 1999.*

Maybe, just maybe, Shakira returned to end her tour in Buenos Aires for a reason other than the insistence of the organizers of the Anfibio Tour. Maybe, just maybe, she returned to the southern city for pleasure and not business.

The various versions of how Shakira met the son of the president of Argentina, Antonio, vary radically, but the majority of Argentine reporters concur that it goes something like this: The first glances and words were exchanged in January of 2000, when she was passing through Buenos Aires fulfilling commitments with one of her sponsors and he was in the middle of political campaign. The magical encounter occurred in a restaurant. "I went to eat with Aníbal Ibarra [a friend and politician] and suddenly, across the room, I saw these eyes… I was caught. I was caught and we started to look at each other. When she got up, I saw her better and I recognized her," Antonio told the Argentine magazine, *Gente*. Then he got up and introduced himself. In that moment, they met, but Shakira had to go back to Miami to get ready for her tour—a tour that included, among others, Antonio's city.

It took a couple more months for the next meeting. During one of her shows in Buenos Aires on the Anfibio tour, to be more precise on the night of March 25, among the spectators in the front rows were the two sons of Fernando de la Rúa, the President of Argentina: Antonio and Aíto. According to reporters, when the concert was over, the two brothers went backstage to congratulate Shakira.

"I love your music," Antonio, the older of the two, is said to have told Shakira. He would say later that he used to listen to her music even before he had met her. "I only wanted to welcome and congratulate you and tell you, um, if you ever return to Argentina I would like to give you some advice on places you can visit in our country. You can't imagine how gorgeous parts of our country are. What do you say?" and like that, with that slightly awkward line, Shakira saw for the second time the son of Argentina's President, a young twenty-six-year-old lawyer and expert in strategic communications. Besides working for the government, Antonio de la Rúa had coordinated the publicity staff that spun his father's presidential campaign, the campaign that won de la Rúa the presidency.

Just exactly how Shakira responded to Antonio in her dressing room was never known, but given the results, it must have been a resounding yes. The singer decided to accept the offer, and a month and a half later she returned to Buenos Aires to finish her tour and take a well-deserved vacation…with Antonio as her "guide." Along with her parents Shakira traveled to San Martín de los Andes and Bariloche, two tourist spots close in the Andes mountains. A bevy of photographers and reporters followed them, prognosticating a romance. The reporters made it their business to know everything: what they were wearing, what they were doing, even what they ate.

After the press reported that Shakira and Antonio had rented a Woody Allen movie and that the following day they did not leave the hotel, Shakira's mom decided it was time to clarify the terms of this new relationship. "They were not on their honeymoon and they never shared the same room," Nidia said, making it very clear that the intimacy of the two ended at bedtime. In any event, the magazines published photographs that demonstrated the obvious chemistry between them.

Beyond the declarations of Nidia Ripoll, the romance between Shakira and the son of the President of Argentina sounded a boom that resounded on an international level. The week that the news broke about the romance, *Shakira* was the sixth most searched word on the search portal AltaVista. And in Colombia, when President de la Rúa arrived in Cartagena for a conference of Latin American presidents, a local newspaper greeted him saying that "Shakira's father-in-law arrives today."

After spending a few days in the southern part of Argentina trying to escape from paparazzi and curious onlookers, Shakira returned to Miami. She had to resume work on the record, which she admitted was behind schedule—nothing new for Shakira. "Shakira Mebarak, the procrastinator" is how she had described herself once, laughing about her own faults. Sony had already reserved Compass Point studios in Nassau, Bahamas, and there she would go with her music and her producers. Legendary recording artists like Bob Marley and the Rolling Stones had once recorded there, and now she would be there working out the rhythms and arrangements to her songs.

Those who were expecting Shakira to emerge from the island with her new album were to be frustrated. After several days of working she announced that she was not finishing up her record, as some sources said, but just starting it. "I have composed several songs for this new album," she said. "But something is still missing, I feel like I have to search deep inside to free some feelings that are trapped." Maybe it was to free those feelings that Antonio de la Rúa went to the Bahamas, very briefly. By this time, he was being called her "boyfriend," even though they were still saying that they were just getting to know each other.

Her relationship with the son of the Argentine president was obvious but was only confirmed when she returned to Miami from the Bahamas. As soon as she got back to Florida, a series of previously scheduled interviews and other commitments awaited her. But between workdays Shakira made time for her Argentine boyfriend, who came to Miami for the sole purpose of seeing her. They went to dinner, spent a few days on the beach, and frolicked in the water. By their side were Nidia, William,...and the paparazzi. The latter were attempting to confirm the romance with their camera lenses, and pictures of the two kissing on the coast of Miami circulated across the globe. The photographers took pictures of them kissing, walking, on the beach, and caressing each other.

As natural as it might be for a romance to bloom between a twenty-three-year-old singer and a twenty-six-year-old lawyer, this was perhaps the most problematic love that the son of the President could have, not so much for him but for his father. These pictures made the cover of every major magazine in Argentina used by some to contrast the "frivolous romance" of the President's son with the drastic salary cuts of more than 140,000 state employees that his father had ordered as part of a reduction in public spending. The timing was unfortunate. These photos provoked a great wave of criticism in his country, since his father had assumed the presidency just a few months before, promising austerity and clarity in his administration. Now, the Argentine press was asking where Antonio was getting the money to travel so much.

But Shakira and "Toñito," as he was called by the magazines, seemed to be experiencing their romance unaware of the reality that surrounded them. She was delaying her next record, and he was ignoring a morass of political problems. Nidia seemed happy with her would-be son-in-law, or at least that's what she told the press. During that time, when neither could deny the obvious, they both acknowledged that they were in love and were a couple. To circumvent nasty rumors, though, while he was in Miami, Antonio stayed at a friend's apartment and not in the Mebaraks' home.

THE FIRST LATIN GRAMMYS: A HISTORIC EVENT

For several years the National Academy of Recording Arts and Sciences (NARAS), the organization in charge of the annual Grammy Awards, had received harsh criticism over the way they grouped Latin artists and how the winners were chosen. There were some industry producers and executives within the organization who were lobbying to create an award ceremony by the Academy exclusively for music in Spanish. As Michael Greene, the president of NARAS, said after seeing Ricky Martin's sensational performance during the ceremony of the Grammy Awards in 1999, "We are prepared to represent more Latin music in our next events." And after twelve years of debate, the new millennium had Michael Greene presenting a new award show that belonged exclusively to Latin music. It would be known as the Latin Grammy Awards, and just like the "classic" Grammy Awards, the winners would be chosen by artists and executives, but of the Latin and Latin American music industry.

This new Grammy would have forty categories, including genres as diverse as pop, rock, ranchera, tango, salsa, merengue, flamenco, and Latin jazz, plus special categories for Brazilian music. This time, there would be no complaints (or so it was believed), as the judges would be musicians and producers with expertise in these genres. And every album would be eligible, no matter where it was recorded, whereas previously the record had to be launched in the United States in order to participate.

The music industry in the United States was recognizing that the Latin market was growing and was sufficiently solid to deserve its own space. It also had the potential audience to make the awards ceremony a televised event: The Latin Grammy Awards would be broadcast on CBS, the same station that broadcasts the traditional Grammys each year, and the program would be bilingual, making it the first bilingual transmission on prime-time television ever.

Two months before the awards show, on July 7, 2000, the names of the nominees in each category were announced. There were many surprises among the finalists announced, especially for those artists outside the United States who had only recently heard about the awards. Shakira received a total of five nominations: "Ojos así" for Best Female Pop Vocal Performance; "Octavo día" for Best Female Rock Vocal Performance; *MTV Unplugged* for Best Pop Album and Album of the Year; and "Inevitable" for Video of the Year.

"OJOS ASÍ"

As proof of the diversity of Latin Music, on September 13, 2000, the most diverse group of artists imaginable paraded through the stage of the Staples Center in Los Angeles. The flamenco guitar of Tomatito, the velvety voice of the Brazilian Djava, and the mariachi music of Alejandro Fernández were all part of the majestic show. The performers made this event a deliciously eclectic reunion, worthy of being called Latin. And the gala was fabulous: an hour before the ceremonies commenced, guests alighted from their limos and sashayed down the red carpet, where they were received by Jon Secada. While this was all happening outside, inside the convention center, presenter Rebecca Rankin made a few announcements about what to expect that evening. Among the artists performing that night, she recommended someone by the name of Shakira, whose rehearsal had left her speechless. Her comment foreshadowed what was to come: Shakira's performance that night would be the most talked about in the press.

The artist arrived in a tight green dress of irregular cut and high boots, with wild blonde hair. She was accompanied by her parents and Antonio de la Rúa, who sat next to her that evening. The ceremony began with a tribute to the late Tito Puente by Celia Cruz, Gloria Estefan, and Ricky Martin, and none other than Sheila E. was on the drums. It was a hot opening for a lively night. The night's hosts, Jimmy Smits, Andy García, and Gloria Estefan, introduced the special guests who would be handing out the awards.

One of the first awards that evening, for Best Female Pop Vocal, went to Shakira for "Ojos así," leaving Christina Aguilera who was nominated for her song "Genio atrapado" (the Spanish version of her hit "Genie in a Bottle"), empty-handed. Shakira was moved, proud, and happy: she walked onto the stage with no notes for a speech and collected her thoughts. She dedicated the award to Colombia, "a country that is going through difficult times right now but that never, never forgets how to smile." And her own smile lit up her face. "This is for you, Colombia."

When she returned to the stage, Shakira was no longer dressed in green nor was she the timid girl who had just accepted an award. Her second appearance at the Latin Grammys was to conquer the stage and do what she does best. Jimmy Smits introduced her with lavish praise, and with that the first chords of "Ojos así" began to fill the center. Opening the performance was a group of dancers dressed as Middle Eastern slaves, offering themselves to the Goddess of the Desert: a blonde in red leather pants and charms around her hips who made her entrance twisting like a snake. Shakira took over the stage like a rebellious odalisque, with sensual movements and the look of a cat. But she didn't stop there. Almost as if justifying her brand-new Grammy, she took the microphone and sang with the fury of a veteran rocker. And whenever she could she did her celebrated belly dance, accenting the "words" of the dumbek. Behind her the stage was filled with flames. Red, yellow, and orange mixed with gold to give her number an unforgettable power. When she finished, the audience, dumbfounded, gave her a standing ovation.

After her performance, Shakira had to endure once again the suspense of the next Latin Grammy award, in which she was nominated for Best Female Rock Vocal for her song "Octavo día." Backstage, Shakira waited and again turned into the timid girl. When her name came from the lips of Jaci Velásquez, the artist could not believe it. She came out, walking rapidly, a little bewildered and racking her brain for what to say. "This one was unexpected." Shakira happily smiled, reflecting back to what she'd said before. "A little while ago when I received my first Grammy...I felt really emotional because I realized how all of you celebrated it with me," and the audience applauded, confirming her words. "Accomplishments are not worth anything if you don't have someone there to share them with," she said, finally finding what she was looking for. "And I have people to share them with." Judging by the force with which the audience applauded, she seemed to have hit on a genuine truth.

The two Latin Grammys are major awards in Shakira's career. They represent the recognition of her peers, and one of the winning songs, "Ojos así," is among of the most visceral and authentic works the artist has ever created. The fusion of the rhythms is very Latin, because as she says, "Latinos are a fusion." However, this song is more than a fusion of pop and oriental rhythms. "Ojos así" is a tribute to her ancestors, and it's the song that showcases her belly dance. That night at the Latin Grammys, when the audience gave her a standing ovation, they were also applauding Shakira's essence: "a combination of elements that come from different worlds but live harmoniously under the same roof." This is what she is, what her music is. And the audience and the viewers at home adored her frankness.

When Shakira says she dreams of visiting Lebanon and singing in front a huge crowd of people, she is serious. She honors her ancestors with her music, dance, and food, and she respects the calling of her blood. When it comes to praying, she prays to the Catholic God and follows the beliefs of her church. She is naturally forgiving, humble, and sensitive. She believes that it is important to use all of the senses, the windows that we humans have into the world. And when she is deeply engaged composing her songs or creating melodies, rebellion strikes and gives her music a rock attitude. That's why she's a self-proclaimed rocker and doesn't care if others say that her music is more pop. She doesn't place herself in one genre or the other. "Pop rock, rock pop, I wouldn't know which to put first," she says. And maybe that is why she prefers to call her music a "fusion" and to define herself as "eclectic."

She is spiritual and she is sensual, even though she doesn't speak overtly about sex. She is religious but also sexy. She is passionate, but also very cerebral. She is a highly demanding and obsessive person when it comes to work, but also willing to listen and learn. Perhaps within all these contradictions lies the wisdom of Shakira. She doesn't deny herself any opportunity to be or to do, always believing in the existence of a Supreme Being that guides her. "I want to see what's on the other side of the river. I'm a woman of challenges and I have to confront them courageously because I don't want to be left thinking, What if?" she said while promoting her Anfibio Tour. Her ultimate goal she does not share, "for fear of being misunderstood." Maybe, just maybe, one of her goals is to become a movie star. She wouldn't be the first singer to follow that path. As a matter of fact, according to *Variety* magazine, she had been considered for roles later given to Catherine Zeta-Jones (in *The Mask of Zorro*, alongside Antonio Banderas) and Penelope Cruz (in *All the Pretty Horses*, alongside Matt Damon). For the latter, Shakira's schedule was so full that she didn't even have time to make the casting call. "I know one day it will happen, it's all about timing," she later told a reporter. But her priority, for now, is her music.

If her goal is to dominate the world as opposed to dominating Hollywood, she is close to achieving it. A month after her impressive performance at the Latin Grammys, *Rolling Stone* dedicated a full page to her, a rarity for a Latin American artist. With two pictures of Shakira in her unforgettable red outfit on September 13, the magazine named her Queen of the Latin Grammys. It reaffirmed her talent as a composer, a quality that sets her apart from "other artists who performed that night, like N'Sync and Christina Aguilera," who are in the majority in the world of teen music. The magazine also quoted the artist when she now famously said, "I don't know if my crossover will be successful, all I know is that I'm going to make a great, great record." And that's what she was doing at the time of the review.

Shakira spent the months of October and November of 2000 on a ranch in Punta del Este in Uruguay, a popular getaway during the southern hemisphere's summer but practically deserted in the spring. Escaping from reporters and photographers, she arrived with her parents at the ranch, close to the beach, far from the highway, thirty minutes away by plane from Buenos Aires, where her boyfriend Antonio lives. In a huge house in the middle of a vast land surrounded by greenery, farm animals, and horses, Shakira waited for the inspiration that was needed to finish her crossover album.

Shakira arrived at the house rented for her by Sony Music (which, according to the Argentine press, cost Sony $25,000) with her parents, her luggage, and a sound board big enough to take up an entire room. A few days later the other musicians and producers began to arrive to resume production of the still untitled album. As with the previous album, this record involved a lot of people. This time, in addition to producers Tim Mitchell, Lester Mendez, Javier Garza, Palo Flores, Luis Fernando Ochoa, and drummer Brendan Buckley, there was a new producer/composer on the team: the renowned Glenn Ballard. If some composers go unnoticed in their collaborations for songs that become hits, this man is not one of them. In the music business, Ballard is not only known for his ability to write number ones with celebrity songwriters like Alanis Morisette and Dave Matthews, but also has the reputation for being an excellent influence on the creative process of the composer with whom he works. Glenn Ballard has been a kind of guru, the "medium" through which some artists find their own voice. The reputation of the charismatic Ballard—and the fact that he worked with Alanis Morissette, the constant comparison to Shakira—is one of the reasons certain people are eagerly anticipating the song he cowrote with the artist.

Meanwhile, in the United States, expectations for the record were growing. Days after the Latin Grammys America Online made Shakira's image available to millions of subscribers when its home page featured her as the great new Latin talent after Ricky Martin. Other Internet sites, in Spanish and English, also dedicated pages to her. Even the online version of *Rolling Stone* ran a complete biography of her on its web site. Thanks to the Internet the support of her fans helped her win MTV's Latin America's People's Choice Award for her video "Ojos así," the video with which she competed in September of that year in the MTV Video Music Awards. Unfortunately, she finished only as a finalist.

By mid-November the popular vote again put her name among the nominees for Best Latin Artist in the American Music Awards for 2001, a distinction she shared with Enrique Iglesias and Marc Anthony. And before that year began the prototype for a Shakira Doll was already underway.

Shakira spent her leisure time in Punta del Este with Antonio. He took the half-hour plane ride from Buenos Aires as often as he could, and stayed for a few days in the Mebarak home. As always her parents, especially her mother, were never far. Nidia had no trouble telling the press that she had traveled to Punta del Este "to keep her company and to chaperone." She told one Argentinean weekly newspaper that she is delighted with her potential future son-in-law. And even though Shakira and Antonio were having an "intense" romance they slept in separate rooms, so that there would be no misunderstandings.

Surrounded by her loves—her parents, her music and Antonio, who was coming and going from Buenos Aires—Shakira spent the last three months of 2000 at the rented farmhouse in Uruguay composing, writing, and working closely with her musicians and producers. The work was intense for, as she says, "I am not easy to work with, I admit." She is so demanding that she preferred to discard the songs that had already been translated into English, including "Inevitable" and "Ojos así," and instead preferred to compose original material, even though this meant more time and sweat.

Shakira had taken her decision to conquer the U.S. market very seriously and every step she'd taken in the last three years had been deliberate—from contacting Emilio Estefan, then Freddy DeMann, and later the producer Glenn Ballard. After winning the two Latin Grammys she knew there was a new audience out there, open and curious, waiting to hear her next record. And she was not going to disappoint them.

When Shakira found out in November that she'd been nominated for an America Music Award (AMA) for Best Latin Artist, she surely knew what it meant for her career. AMA nominees are chosen by the music industry based on a popularity poll and the winners are elected by a direct popular vote. For a newcomer to the U.S. market, the nomination was in itself an award. "This is a vote of confidence from my American fans and it comes at a special time for me," she said. It was the first time Shakira had been nominated for this quintessentially American award and she shared the honor with no less than Marc Anthony and Enrique Iglesias. That her level of popularity was rising was obvious, and that was one more incentive (or pressure) to produce the best material possible. "I want to make a great album, with honest songs and good music," she told the news agency Notimex. "I've written thirty songs, some in English, others in Spanish, and I'm extremely excited about the way they're coming out," she concluded.

Beyond those sporadic statements to the press, Shakira has stayed pretty well isolated on the ranch. Her manager and her record label conspired to prevent her from granting interviews until she finished the record, which at that point they were still hoping could come out by Spring, sometime between March and June of 2001. Whether the record was going to be all English or part English/part Spanish, was still unknown at the end of 2000. Proving Shakira's uncommon level of freedom, neither Sony Music nor Estefan Enterprises could say for sure if the artist was going to include a few songs in Spanish. It was only in March that Sony could say for sure that the record would be 80 percent English, 20 percent Spanish.

When December arrived, Shakira packed up. After three months of total immersion in her work, the time had come to leave that "womb of creativity" on the Uruguayan coast and go home. Shakira went back to Miami to organize all the material she'd created, and also to pack new bags. A few days after returning home, she met up with Antonio again to take a deserved vacation. Together they flew to Vienna, then Morocco, according the Argentine magazine *Gente*. According to *Gente*, Shakira and Antonio spent their first Christmas together alone in Casablanca, the romantic city where Ingrid Bergman fell in love with Humphrey Bogart. And there must truly be something magic in that corner of the world because when they returned from vacation, both appeared relaxed, smiling, and more in love than ever. Upon their return from Morocco, in early 2001, neighbors reported they had both taken to wearing white Moroccan tunics. For Shakira, the Morocco period lasted a while: as January unfolded, it was common to see her on Miami's Millionaire Road, on the way to her recording studio, in that tunic, and in sandals with socks. She was also often seen with a little white puppy named Cupid, which Antonio had given her for Christmas.

But Antonio couldn't go everywhere with Shakira. In January, when the artist traveled to Barranquilla for the wedding of one her brothers, she went without a date. It was a quick trip; according to *TV y Novelas*, Shakira was in and out in a day, long enough to attend her older brother Alberto's wedding and to spend the day with her father's side of the family. The party barely over, Shakira was en route back to Miami, to her house and more important, to her work. The clock was ticking.

Naturally, though, even in her packed schedule, she did manage to clear a few hours to celebrate her birthday. February 2 started with Antonio's arrival. He flew in from Buenos Aires bearing flowers and a teddy bear. She ended the day in the popular restaurant, Bongos, in a party that her promoter, Jairo Martínez, had planned and that lasted until five in the morning. Her friends, parents, and her little entertainment circle in Miami were all there, along with her boyfriend of a year now.

On the eve of the highly anticipated crossover, there was another surprise awaiting Shakira—perhaps the best so far. The American Music Awards were awarded on January 8 in the Shrine Auditorium in Los Angeles. This time, Enrique Iglesias won Favorite Latin Artist in the United States, leaving Shakira and Marc Anthony empty-handed. But that defeat didn't keep her down, since five days earlier she'd received a nomination for the most important award in the music industry: the gold one, the one in the shape of a gramophone, the dream of every music professional.

On January 3, the day Shakira returned to Miami from Morocco, the nominees of the 43rd Annual Grammy Awards were announced, in Beverly Hills, California. Shakira was nominated for Best Latin Pop Album for *MTV Unplugged*. Sharing the category were the romantic Luis Miguel for *Vivo;* the seductive Alejandro Sanz for *El alma al aire;*the boxer-turned singer Oscar De la Hoya; and Christina Aguilera, who was competing again against Shakira with *Mi reflejo.*

This was Shakira's second Grammy nomination. Two years earlier, the Grammy had gone to the Mexican group Maná, so she did not want to raise her hopes. But this second nomination found Shakira in a more promising place: she'd already won two Latin Grammys, one of which she'd taken from the almost-ubiquitous Christina Aguilera, and her popularity was on the rise in the U.S. Perhaps this popularity rise was best seen in the media. In February, for example, *The Wall Street Journal* spoke of Shakira as the Latin model of the new global culture. In the prestigious newspaper, Bruce Orwall briefly summarized her career and reported on the preparations to turn her Latin American success into a North American success, the way she was able to add to her talent the wise advice of star-makers like Emilio Estefan, Tommy Mottola, and Freddy DeMann. Shakira's popularity was compared to other cultural phenomena that caught fire in the United States, like *Survivor,* or the Japanese "Pokémon," or the bestselling Harry Potter books. But in the case of a singer-songwriter, the reporter pointed out, such a globalization meant risking the loss of the core market—in Shakira's case, the Latin American market.

But Shakira had already processed those risks and was powering full steam ahead, leaving behind the fear of losing touch with her roots. "I am going to make an honest record," she had vowed again and again. And this left her with a clear conscience. That was her goal and that's why she had spent so many months absorbed in her work. At that point, she'd finished fifteen songs in English and she said she was in love with fifteen of them. Coming from someone so demanding, the record sounded promising.

So Shakira had a chance to win the Grammy that twenty-first of February 2001. But because of the previous loss, she arrived at the Staples Center expecting to lose. "We try to keep really low expectations to avoid that dashed hopes syndrome," she told the press after the ceremony. She wore a tight and sexy gold dress that night, another design by the Argentine María Vázquez, and she walked in calmly holding hands with Antonio de la Rúa. Most of the TV cameras covering the red carpet overlooked Shakira's arrival. They were mesmerized by Christina Aguilera, the members of Destiny's Child, and Shelby Lynn. Among the performances that night, the most anticipated was the controversial duet between Eminem and Elton John. Madonna, Mobi, and Christina Aguilera also performed, but none of those three won. The night belonged to U2, and an incredulous Bono, and Steely Dan, the duo who practically owned the seventies and eighties and who had made a comeback with new material. It also turned out to be Shakira's night—though she could hardly believe it either.

When Shakira heard her name called from the stage to come up and accept her Grammy, her eyes opened like plates. She couldn't believe it. She was so surprised that she looked around waiting for someone to tell her it was all a joke. But it was serious, of course, and she did not know how to react. "It was like an inner earthquake, like drowning; I couldn't catch my heart rate," she told the Colombian newspaper *El Tiempo*. But it didn't take long to compose herself, let go of Antonio's hand, and walk quickly up to the stage. She felt awkward, she was afraid she would trip over her dress and fall to the floor. And when she finally reached the stage and took that precious trophy in her hands, she was so moved that she was speechless. Possibly out of superstition, she hadn't prepared a speech. She was radiant, happy, thrilled, and you could tell. The words finally came like the fruit of her emotion: she shared this award with Antonio, "the love of my life," with the people who had helped her, and with her entire Latin American audience. Again, she dedicated the award to her country and her people. And to them, she gave a rousing "Viva Colombia!"—perhaps the only Spanish words spoken at the ceremony, a cry that sprang from her gut and that clearly demonstrated where her heart was.

Her country responded with the same love. In Colombia, this Grammy was celebrated like a World Cup Soccer victory. They actually played the National Anthem on the air while Shakira was accepting her award. The next day she and her award dominated the headlines of every newspaper in the country and a few days later the covers of every important magazine. Clearly in her native land she continued to be a heroine, a source of national pride, and, to many, a role model—all this even though she was about to switch languages on her next album. Such a positive response to this Grammy throughout Colombia was perhaps the most convincing evidence that Shakira would not lose the audience that had been with her all these years.

But the euphoria of the Grammy didn't last long. The next day, with next to no sleep, Shakira flew back to Miami to get back to work on wrapping up the album. At that point she had fifteen songs from which she could only choose twelve for the album. A hard choice. Many of these songs were dedicated to Antonio, in whom she seemed to have found the love of her life. The couple was looking more committed with every passing month, and the relationship seemed to grow in importance despite the distances and the demanding work schedules. But Shakira is never one to get ahead of herself, especially not with respect to a relationship. Whenever the press asked when she thought she might get married, she always answered "not at the moment." Despite experiencing the greatest romance of her life, her career still came first, or at least it was more demanding.

By early April of 2001, Shakira was taking the first practice bounces on the diving board of her next album. She was just about to take the dive and expectations were high. She'd prepared with the best trainers and was in superior shape physically The pool, in turn, was full. The spectators were alert. The press was waiting too. All there was left to do was watch the mastery of the great dive.

DISCOGRAPHY

Magia, 1991 (released only in Colombia)

1. Sueños
2. Esta noche voy contigo
3. Lejos de tu amor
4. Magia
5. Cuentas conmigo
6. Cazador de amor
7. Necesito de ti
8. Tus gafas oscuras

Peligro, 1993 (released only in Colombia)

1. Eres
2. Último momento
3. Tú serás la historia de mi vida
4. Peligro
5. Quince años
6. Brujería
7. Eterno amor

8. Controlas mi destino

9. Este amor es lo más bello del mundo

10. 1968

Pies descalzos, 1995

1. Estoy aquí

2. Antología

3. Un poco de amor

4. Quiero

5. Te necesito

6. Vuelve

7. Te espero sentada

8. Pies descalzos, sueños blancos

9. Pienso en ti

10. Dónde estás corazón?

11. Se quiere, se mata

Shakira, The Remixes, 1997

1. Shakira DJ Megamix

2. Estoy aquí

3. Estou aqui

4. Dónde estás corazón? (dance remix)

5. Un poco de amor (extended dancehall mix)

6. Um pouco de amor

7. Pies descalzos, sueños blancos (Meme's super club mix)

8. Pés delcalços

9. Estoy aquí

10. Dónde estás corazón?

11. Un poco de amor (Meme's jazz experience)

12. Pies descalzos, sueños blancos (The timbalero dub 97)

Dónde están los ladrones?, 1998

1. Ciega sordomuda
2. Si te vas
3. Moscas en la casa
4. No creo
5. Inevitable
6. Octavo día
7. Que vuelvas
8. Tú
9. Dónde están los ladrones?
10. Sombra de ti
11. Ojos así

Shakira, MTV Unplugged, 2000

1. Octavo día
2. Si te vas
3. Dónde están los ladrones?
4. Moscas en la casa
5. Ciega sordomuda
6. Inevitable
7. Estoy aquí
8. Tú
9. Sombra de ti
10. No creo
11. Ojos así

The lyrics to these songs can be found on the Internet, on one of the many Shakira fan sites.

Try http://www.donde-esta-shakira.com/lyrics/.

AWARDS AND RECOGNITIONS

GRAMMY AWARD, 2001
Best Latin Pop Album, *MTV Unplugged*

PREMIOS LO NUESTRO, 2001
Rock Album of the Year, *MTV Unplugged*
Rock Performance of the Year

BILLBOARD LATIN MUSIC AWARDS, 2001
Nomination: Pop Album of the Year, Female, *MTV Unplugged*
Nomination: Billboard Latin 50 Artist of the Year
Nomination: Latin Rock Album of the Year, *MTV Unplugged*

AMERICAN MUSIC AWARDS, 2001
Nomination: Best Latin Music Artist

LATIN GRAMMY AWARDS, 2000
Best Female Rock Vocal Performance, "Octavo día"
Best Female Pop Vocal Performance, "Ojos así"
Other nominations: Album of the Year and Best Pop Album, *MTV Unplugged*; Best Music Video, "Ojos así"

PEOPLE'S CHOICE AWARDS, MTV LATIN AMERICA, 2000

Favorite Video, "Ojos así"

GRAMMY AWARD, 1999

Nomination: Best Latin Rock/Alternative Vocal Performance for *Dónde están los ladrones?*

PREMIO AMIGO, ESPAÑA, 1999

Best Latin-American Solo Artist

PREMIO MTV LATINOAMÉRICA, 1999

Voted second Best Singer of the 90's

PREMIOS LO NUESTRO, 1999

Best Pop Artist, Female

Best Pop Album for *Dónde están los ladrones?*

COLOMBIAN ARTIST OF THE CENTURY

Revista *TV y Novelas*

BILLBOARD LATIN MUSIC AWARDS, 1999

Best Female Pop Artist, *Dónde están los ladrones?*

BILLBOARD, DECEMBER, 1998

#1, Latin Top 50

PREMIO ERES, MEXICO, 1998

Best Female Pop Performance

WORLD MUSIC AWARDS, MÓNACO, 1998

Best Latin Artist

GOOD WILL AMBASSADOR

Colombian President Ernesto Samper, Colombia, 1998

SUPER CONGO DE ORO, 1998

Carnaval de Barranquilla

SONY MUSIC, MAY 1997

Multi-platinum Record for *Pies descalzos*

PREMIOS LO NUESTRO, 1997

Best Female Pop Artist

Best New Artist

BILLBOARD LATIN MUSIC AWARDS, 1997

Best Album for *Pies descalzos*

Best Video for "Estoy aquí"

Best New Artist

PRISMA DE DIAMANTE, SONY/COLOMBIA, 1996

Diamond Prism (one million albums sold) for *Pies descalzos*

PREMIO DE REVISTA *TV Y NOVELAS*, COLOMBIA, 1994

Best National Artist

FESTIVAL DE VIÑA DEL MAR, CHILE, 1993

Third place award with song "Eres"

SHAKIRA
ON THE WEB

These are a few of the best sites where information about Shakira can be found:

http://www.shakiramebarak.com/
http://www.angelfire.com/co/shakira/
http://www.shakira-mebarak.itgo.com/
http://www.shakiravideo.cjb.net/
http://shakimeba.webjump.com/
http://www.geocities.com/ojosasi_mx/
http://www.donde-esta-shakira.com/
http://shakira.metropoli2000.net
http://www.shakiromaniacos.cjb.net/
http://www.telenovelas-internet.com/special/shakira031300/shak.html
http://www.mundo21.com/musica/bios/shakira.php3

BIBLIOGRAPHY

Cambio, En primera persona, Shakira, by Gabriel García Márquez

Cromos, February 24, 1997; February 26, 2001

Diario de Hoy, El Salvador, May 2000

El Espacio, Colombia, June 7, 1997, and August 1, 1998

Gente magazine, March 1998; October 24, 2000; October 2000;
    January 30, 2001

El Heraldo, April 8, 2000

Latin Music and Entertainment Magazine, September/October 1999

Latina, April 1999

Miami Herald, July 8, 2000

Mtvl.com

People en Español, June/July 1999

Revista Semana, May19–26, 1997; February 26, 2001

Ritmo de la Noche, June/July 2000

Rolling Stone, October 26, 2000

Semana.com, September 2000

Seventeen, August 2000

Shakira, Ojos Así, by Estheban Reynoso

Shock magazine, 1998

Sonicnet.com

Sonymusic.com

Telenovelas Internet, ¿Dónde estás, Shakira?, by Nol Cirene Molina

El Tiempo, October 12, 1997; May 8, 1998; September 20, 1998; February 23, 2001

Time.com, August 3, 1998

TV y Novelas de Colombia, Número Especial de Shakira (Special Issue on Shakira) and February 26 to March 11, 2001

El Universal, April 15, 1997; May 15, 1997

The Wall Street Journal, February 13, 2001

About the Author

●●●
•••

Born in Buenos Aires, Argentina, in 1970, Ximena Diego studied advertising and journalism. After working five years in advertising and marketing, she decided journalism was her calling. Her life took a 180 degree turn after she came to New York with the pretext of continuing her studies. Almost accidentally, she met her future husband and began to publish her first articles.

She began to write articles for *Impacto Latin News,* covering entertainment news and interviewing celebrities from the Latin culture. From there she worked for the bilingual *Latina* magazine, where she did translations and collaborated on several articles. Ximena could not resist the temptation of the dot.coms and is currently working as entertainment editor at StarMedia, a Spanish and Portuguese search portal for Latin America and Spain.